Women on the
the
Edge

Cindi McMenamin

HARVEST HOUSE PUBLISHERS

EUGENE, OREGON

Cover photo © Stellapictures/Brand X Pictures/Getty Images

Cover by Dugan Design Group, Bloomington, Minnesota

WOMEN ON THE EDGE
Copyright © 2010 by Cindi McMenamin
Published by Harvest House Publishers
Eugene, Oregon 97402
www.harvesthousepublishers.com

Library of Congress Cataloging-in-Publication Data

McMenamin, Cindi, 1965-
   Women on the edge / Cindi McMenamin.
      p. cm.
   Includes bibliographical references.
   ISBN 978-0-7369-2652-2 (pbk.)
   1. Christian women—Religious life. 2. Desire for God. I. Title.
BV4527.M3355 2010
248.8'43—dc22

                             2009047448

Printed in the United States of America

10 11 12 13 14 15 16 17 18 / BP-SK / 10 9 8 7 6 5 4 3 2 1

For every woman who has ever felt like she was on the edge.
I've been there.
And so has the Lover of your soul.

You, LORD, are all I want!
You are my choice, and you keep me safe.
You make my life pleasant, and my future is bright.

PSALM 16:5-6 CEV

Acknowledgments

My heartfelt thanks to:

- My husband, Hugh, and daughter, Dana, for their patience and unconditional love for a wife and mother who many times seems on the edge.

- My friend Chris, for bringing light and hope to this book through her beautiful testimony.

- My friend Ashley, for laughing with me and encouraging me to keep writing whenever I was feeling on the edge.

- My friend and sister in ministry, Kelly Bell, for encouraging me to write for women who feel desperate.

- My friend Patti, whose new relationship with Jesus reminds me once again of the joys of discovering Him and what it means to be desperate for God.

- My speaking audiences and readers—across the nation and overseas—who have poured out their hearts in sharing their stories, frustrations, insights, and joys about what it truly means to be women on the edge.

And above all, I'm grateful to my Lord and Savior Jesus Christ for "showing great kindness when I was like a city under attack" (Psalm 31:21 CEV).

Contents

Standing at the Crossroads

I will praise you, LORD, for showing great kindness
when I was like a city under attack.

PSALM 31:21 CEV

Shari felt like a city under attack.

Her two teenagers showed little respect for her in their words and actions. And her husband, after 22 years of marriage, still seemed to side with the kids. She felt unappreciated, unsupported, disrespected, extremely frustrated. Shari was on the edge.

I can't live this way anymore, she told herself aloud as she drove home from work. She had had enough. She was tired of the tension that awaited her at home, weary of the battles, discouraged by her failed attempts to talk about her frustrations and convinced they would continue to fall on deaf ears. She desperately wanted to run. She desperately wanted to change her situation, but didn't know how. She needed to talk, but felt no one would understand. Deep in her heart she loved her family, yet she felt—in that moment—that she never wanted to see them again.

As she neared her home, she relived the pain and frustration of a conflict the night before. Mentally planning her escape, she arrived at home, intending to pack her bags and go wherever the road took her.

Upon arriving at the house, Shari went into her bedroom and began to pack. Her mind was swirling. She could barely think straight. She was so weary of unresolved conflict. A lump formed in her throat at the thought of really leaving. *This is wrong,* a voice in her head whispered. "But to stay miserable is okay?" she questioned herself, aloud.

Just make them miss you for awhile so they'll rethink how they've been treating you, she thought. But this was not who she wanted to be. Shari crumpled to the floor and began to cry.

7

"I want to leave, God!" she shouted. "But I have nowhere to go. I love them, but I can't live with them any longer!"

Shari had finally arrived at the crossroads—the place where life's expectations and life's reality crash together painfully. A place where the pain seems overwhelming and the road of escape seems to promise relief. A place where she is truly on the edge of making either a wise or foolish decision. She had a choice: She could follow her desires toward destruction or toward a destiny of delight.

Such crossroads are nothing new. God gave this instruction to His people centuries ago:

> Stand at the crossroads and look; ask for the ancient paths,
> ask where the good way is, and walk in it,
> and you will find rest for your souls (Jeremiah 6:16).

Shari needed to know "where the good way is" and she needed the strength to walk in it. She took a deep breath and asked one of the most important questions a woman can ask when she is teetering on the edge: "God, what do *You* want me to do?"

After a good cry on the floor, Shari picked herself up and pleaded with God to change her heart.

> *God, give me a discerning heart to know how to talk to my teenagers...to know how to unconditionally love them, not so they will take advantage of me, but so they will be convicted by their behavior and learn to love unconditionally as well.*
>
> *God, give me discernment to view my husband's actions so I will see the best in him, not the worst. Show me what he's doing right so that I will not always focus on his failures as a dad and husband.*
>
> *God, change me so I will behave in such a way that I draw out loving responses from the rest of my family.*

With Shari's prayer came not immediate results, but immediate peace. She began to trust that the One who is bigger, stronger, and much more powerful than her could work out this situation and walk her calmly away from the edge to a spacious place of love and grace.

Upon arriving at the crossroads (and while she was packing her bags), Shari believed she was choosing survival and sanity over continued pain and frustration. But Shari may not have realized that two paths were looming before her—the path of following her own desires (for change, fulfillment, peace, happiness), which would eventually lead to her demise (feelings of abandonment and betrayal from her husband and children, isolation, possibly divorce), or the path of obedience to God by asking what *He* wanted of her life, which would lead to freedom and fulfillment.

Like Shari, we all feel—at one time or another—like a "city under attack." We find ourselves on the edge, in need of a spacious place of understanding and unconditional love. We all stand at the crossroads at certain points in our life and ask ourselves:

> *Is this all there is in life?*
>
> *Don't I deserve something better than what I have now?*
>
> *Why am I putting up with all of this?*
>
> *Do I really want life to turn out the way it's continuing to go?*
>
> *Might I be happier if I just left this situation?*

Sometimes we feel better when we blow our top, have an emotional meltdown, or just walk away. But we all, at one time or another, find ourselves at a crossroads where we must decide whether our desperation will rule us or we will rule it.

Like Shari, I know what it's like to feel like I'm teetering on the edge. I have those days when I'm not just disappointed, not merely disillusioned, but feeling downright desperate. Desperate for change. Desperate for control. Desperate to feel respected, appreciated, cherished. I can relate to the *I've got to get out of this situation now before I have a complete meltdown* kind of desperate. The *if things don't change I'm going to go crazy* kind of desperate.

I've been told it's a midlife thing. I've been told it's hormonal. I've been told it's just life. But I've never been told I'm alone in feeling this way. Just about every woman I talk to has encountered situations that make her feel like she's losing her mind. And I'm guessing you have, too, because you've picked up this book and read this far. After surveying nearly 100 women from different ages and stages in life—as well as talking with, discipling, and counseling hundreds of other women over the past ten years as a pastor's wife, Bible teacher, and national speaker—I'm convinced that *every* woman feels desperate at one time or another. *Every* woman has experienced a kind of passion about something that has turned into a feeling of desperation. *Every* woman has felt that feeling of being on the edge.

But desperation in and of itself isn't necessarily a bad thing. It all depends on what we're desperate *for*.

Although there are days when my desperation focuses inwardly upon me, there are also times when my desperation drives me to a deeper desire for what is good and pure and right. For example, I am desperate for God to have a bigger influence on my life. I am desperate for more harmony in my marriage. I am desperate for my teenager to love God and want to serve Him with her whole heart. I am desperate for a more holy life. I am desperate to reach women who are dying without a saving knowledge of Jesus Christ.

As you look at that list you may wonder, "What's so bad about being desperate? As long as I'm desperate for *those* kinds of things, God can do a great work in my life."

It's when I begin to be desperate for *other things* that the danger lurks. When I'm desperate for control over a situation or desperate to be happy, fulfilled, or loved. When I'm desperate to be noticed, desperate to find myself, desperate to accomplish, or desperate to have something that God has withheld from me, that's when my desperation becomes dangerous. And if that desperation is not directed in a healthy direction, it can lead to destruction. Yet...

> if I'm desperate for more of *something* and let God turn that into a desperation for more of *Him*...
>
> if I'm desperate to be *happy*, and let God direct that into a desperation to *please Him*...
>
> if I'm desperate to be *loved*, and let God direct that toward a more passionate *love for Him*...
>
> if I'm desperate to *accomplish* and let God steer that toward a desire for *Him* to be glorified...

then I am letting *God* direct my destiny toward delight. I am letting Him show me "where the good way is" so I can walk in it.

You, too, have the capacity to let God turn *your* desperation into a desire for Himself that will change the course of your destiny and lead you not to destruction, but to a destiny of delight.

Perhaps, like me, you can relate to being a woman on the edge when it comes to...

- desperately wanting intimacy in your marriage (or a man to be intimate with!)

- desperately wanting to have a child (or wanting your children to walk with God)

- desperately wanting peace in your home (or just wanting a home)

- desperately wanting to avoid the patterns of the past

- desperately wanting joy and fulfillment in your life

- desperately wanting to be understood and known for who you really are

- desperately wanting to live life with a sense of purpose

- desperately wanting to please God

- desperately wanting to make a difference in your home, community, or world

- desperately wanting to accomplish a dream that hasn't yet come to fruition

Any of those desperations can lead you down a destructive detour in life or toward a deeper desire for God. I'm convinced there's no road in between. So the issue is a serious one. Where do you want to go with *your* passion? Which road do *you* want to follow? What do *you* want to do with your moments (or seasons) of desperation? They can bring you down or raise you up. They can lead to sin or to serving God with a stronger passion. They can cause you to falter or to flourish.

Through the pages of this book, I will show you how you can take the sources of desperation in your life and turn them into a deeper desire for God. On our journey, we'll look at the Bible's recorded history of real-life women who were teetering on the edge. I will show you who let God win, and who continued to struggle. We'll also look at women today who stood at the crossroads and wondered which path to choose. And somewhere in there, you will find yourself—a woman who still has the choice to either let her desperations lead her toward destruction, or let God direct her desires toward a destiny of delight. In their stories, you may find your own. And in the choices they've faced—and are still facing—I'm certain you'll see the choices that compete for your attention as well. Finally, in the strength they continue to find each day, I trust you'll find your anchor of hope so you can stay grounded, and your source of strength so you can move forward.

Come with me, my friend, as we discover that spacious place where we can dwell so we are no longer women on the edge. Come with me on the path that enables us to not just walk, but race toward freedom and fulfillment. Join me as we develop such a desperation for God that we will be living on the edge for *Him*.

After all—as the passionate women that we are—if we're gonna be desperate, we may as well be desperate for God!

Part One

Surviving on the Edge

DESPERATIONS THAT CAN DEVASTATE

Longings within the heart of a woman can become
desperations that drive her toward destruction—or
detours that lead her toward a delightful destiny.

Let's examine the desperations of our hearts that take us
to the edge and, in them, find the One to whom we can
cling...and the spacious place where we can be free.

1

Desperate for More

DESIRING GOD ALONE

You're blessed when you're at the end of your rope.
With less of you there is more of God and his rule.

MATTHEW 5:3 MSG

One thing I ask of the LORD, this is what I seek:
that I may dwell in the house of the LORD all the days of my life,
to gaze upon the beauty of the LORD
and to seek him in his temple.

PSALM 27:4

Lara seemed to have it all. She had a husband and children who loved her, a beautiful home, many friends, and a promising future. She was the kind of woman everyone wanted to be around because of her optimism and energy.

I met Lara at a season in her life in which she was ready for more. Desperate for more. Although I didn't realize how desperate. All of her children were finally out of the house and either married or established in their careers. She'd served in her church alongside her husband for several years, being the wind beneath his wings. Now she felt it was *her* turn.

We met regularly and talked often about her next step in ministry. She wanted her life to count. She wanted her story—of incredible things that God had done in her life—to be heard. We talked about what she was ready for God to do in her life. I began to mentor her in speaking and we talked about writing her book. All seemed to be going well.

Then one day everything changed.

The Lara I knew was gone. Literally. She left her marriage and ministry.

She left her family and friends. She left her responsibilities and reputation. She was desperate for something and she, heartbreakingly, chose a path that hurt everyone who ever knew her—or *thought* they knew her. I tried to contact her, and she texted back that she was "fine." I tried to set up a meeting, and she changed her phone number. I tried to hunt her down, and she remained elusive.

What had happened? What went wrong? And how could I have not seen it coming?

Yet somehow, I did.

Underneath the energy and enthusiasm of this woman was the gnawing hunger for something more. But I brushed it off as normal female talk. All women talk jokingly of what they could experience if they were single again, of where they could be in life if they weren't tied down with children, of what more they could be doing if they had more money, or of what life certainly owes them by now, *don't they?* All women vent now and then about how they've had it with all their responsibilities, all their hard work, and all the expectations placed upon them by everyone they know. All women sound, every now and then, like they're ready to fly the coop. So why are we so surprised when they finally do?

My heart aches today with the realization that nearly every week for almost a year I was sitting across the table from a woman on the edge—on the edge of truly making a difference for God, or spiraling downward toward self destruction. She had two paths in front of her: the path toward life and blessings, or the path toward destruction. She, perhaps unknowingly, chose destruction. And I was powerless to intervene.

You and I, at times, are Lara, too. One minute we love life and others are feeding off of our energy. The next minute we are so weighed down with responsibilities, burdens, heartaches, or frustrations that we want to run—far away from anything that threatens to hold us down. One minute we appear happy and content with what life has brought us, and the next we are ready to dump it all and start over. Deep within us is a well that constantly screams for more.

Every day, in some way, two paths loom before us. One lures us with the fantasy of escape—a lie promising a life of less responsibility and less struggle. The other path doesn't promise ease, but eternal fulfillment and joy if we put aside our desire for immediate pleasure and focus on long-term joy. I often have to ask myself, "Which one will I take?" Do

I long for blessings God's way…or will I insist on getting them in my own way? Do I long for life the way God designed and intended it? Or will I attempt to carve out my own path, not realizing it will lead to a destructive end?

There are many "paths" that seem right to a woman, which we'll look at throughout this book. But the end result is often pain—emotional, spiritual, and sometimes even physical pain. One of those paths includes wanting more because we believe we deserve it.

As humans, we are wired to want more. As women, we *long* for more. But what is at the core of our longing for more? And why does that longing turn to desperation and make us feel we're on the edge? I believe our longings for more started with the first woman to ever walk this earth—and the first woman to ever be given a choice.

Why Is More Never Enough?

Eve was a woman who had it all. Literally. She was married to Mr. Perfect. (Adam was the mold for masculinity, the ideal man formed in the likeness of God.) Besides having a perfect husband, Eve had a beautiful garden home (that never needed weeding!), no noisy (or nosey) neighbors, no job pressures on her or her husband, no debts or bills to pay, no in-laws, and no disobedient or demanding children. She didn't even have laundry! (Because they were naked before the Fall, remember?)

Yep, Eve had the perfect life. Not only was her life perfect, but *she* was perfect. No complaints about her health, her looks, her body, her weight, her hair. She was perfect and complete in every way. She and her husband experienced the perfect life in a perfect place with nothing but time to relish in the enjoyment of their world, their Creator, and each other. They were living one continuous honeymoon in Paradise. What a life! But for some reason, it wasn't enough for her.

We don't know how long Eve relished the beauty and bliss of her existence, living in close companionship with her husband and her Creator. Was it a few days, a week, a month? Or was it only a matter of a few hours? We do know that when Satan came along in the form of a serpent and pointed out to Eve something that she *didn't* have, Eve felt for the first time a desire for something more. The serpent told her if she ate the fruit of the tree of the knowledge of good and evil, "your eyes will be opened, and you will be like God, knowing good and evil" (Genesis 3:5). To be the crown of God's creation apparently wasn't enough. Eve wanted to be *like God*. Her role as "*the* Woman"—the only woman on earth, and perfect at that!—wasn't enough. She wanted more.

When the serpent told her that her eyes would be opened and she would know the difference between good and evil, it appealed to her. She wanted her eyes to be "opened." Consider the beauty Eve's eyes had access to already: A breathtakingly beautiful garden with colors more vivid than anything we can imagine; a perfect, unblemished world without weeds or wilted leaves or dried up grass or any sign of death. Yet she wanted more.

Scripture says when Eve saw the fruit "was good for food [she wanted to taste it] and pleasing to the eye [she wanted to have what she saw] and also desirable for gaining wisdom,"[1] she wanted more. Eve had been given a perfectly sound mind. She could reason. She could point out to Satan his error and embellishment when he asked, "Did God really say, 'You must not eat from any tree in the garden'?" She was able to repeat back to him God's command. But she wanted to know what she didn't know. Evidently the thought of having more wisdom than she already had must have pulled at her.

Oh, why didn't Eve trust God with what He had given her? What if she had not listened to that tempting voice that told her she'd be happier if she just had *more*? What if she had responded to the tempter by saying, "I don't need to know evil; God has given me all that I need to be happy in my relationship with Him"?

Couldn't she be satisfied with God's goodness toward her and choose not to believe He was holding out on her? What if Eve had responded by saying, "That doesn't sound like something my Master would do…withhold from me what I truly desire. I will take this matter before the One who has my best at heart." We learn from the story that that person was not her husband. Adam, too, succumbed to the temptation. Eve sought more *apart* from God. And she sought the safety of numbers by including her husband in her sin.

Couldn't she be satisfied with knowing that God had already given her all the wisdom she would ever need? Yet she wanted more.

When Satan made Eve aware of something she *didn't* have, she became desperate to have it. She actually brought God's goodness and love for her into question when she began to ponder the fact that God had withheld something from her. In fact, Scripture says she looked and saw that something was "good" (in her own judgment, apparently) and partook of it. When she took that forbidden fruit, wanting more for herself than her Maker considered best for her, she ended up losing it all. She lost her home, her health, her happiness, her perfect unity with her husband, her unblemished intimacy with God, and ultimately her life on earth. Eve's desperation for more led to a destiny of spiritual and physical death. Looking back now, was that one piece of fruit in the garden worth risking—and losing—it all? Was the desire for a little more worth losing everything?

We need to ask ourselves that question, too.

Our Unquenchable Longing

You and I are so like Eve. We, too, have been given so much, but we often believe if we had something more, we'd be happier. Like Eve, we too seek company and safety in numbers. *If someone will do this with me (if someone will give me their blessing, if someone will tell me it's not wrong for me to be feeling this way), then it must not be that bad.*

Eve's desire for more, apart from God, led to isolation—isolation from God and from the garden. Isolation, at times, from her husband, whom she knew complete unity with before she had ventured to get more. Her desperation for more led to devastation—living in a cursed world, as well as death for her and for all who would come after her. The stakes were extremely high. And she risked, and lost, it all. It's ironic that Eve's desire for *more* resulted in her losing *everything* she had.

What About You?

Do you know what it's like to hear the Tempter do a number on you, as well? I do. Instead of tempting me to eat fruit that will supposedly make me wise, he changes the words a bit and makes it look like a whole different approach. But really, it's the same strategy he used with Eve. His lines sound something like this (can you relate to these whispers from the enemy as well?):

> "For the first time in your life, why don't you think about *you*, instead of everyone else?"

> "You shouldn't have to put up with that anymore. You deserve far better."

"Who says that's off limits? Go ahead. You won't hurt anyone. And nobody else has to know."

"Why shouldn't you have something like that? You've spent your life making sure everyone else has what *they* want."

"You should know what it's like to partake in that. Then you'll be better able to minister to others who are struggling with it."

"Go ahead...live for the moment. It's really not that big of a deal."

The lies are the same. They imply that God does *not* have your best interest at heart when it comes to your lot in life and your circumstances. Those lies imply that God is not a good God when it comes to the boundaries He drew for you. They call God a liar. Yet the Bible says, "No good thing does he withhold from those whose walk is blameless" (Psalm 84:11).

What are *you* longing for right now? Do you lack a husband, or one whom you can trust? Do you lack a child, or one who will obey, or a job that will pay, or a purpose that will satisfy? What has God already blessed you with? And what might He be withholding for your own good?

Unfortunately, I am like Eve sometimes. I have been given *so* much. And yet I often find myself not only desiring more, but *asking God* for more!

Focusing on the One Thing

Recently I went to God in prayer with my shopping list of what I was truly desperate for.

> *God, there are so many things on my heart right now. I'm concerned about this financial matter that seems to be pressing in on us. And then there's my daughter's MRI this afternoon, which will show us if she has to have another surgery on her knee. And my daughter should've had a call for a film audition by now. Please remember her in that, Lord, so she doesn't get discouraged. And Lord, I really need peace about a disappointment in my life that is causing me to become restless. And God, there's*

a certain area of my life in which you know I am restless. God,
would you bring about the desired changes so I can be happy
and at peace?

My list was long, and I was exhausted after recounting it all to God.
Then my devotional reading that morning took me to Psalm 27—a psalm
I'd read many times, and taught, as well. But this time, it seemed to read
differently to me—as a gentle reminder, or maybe even a rebuke:

> *One* thing I ask of the LORD, *this* is what I seek: That I may
> dwell in the house of the LORD all the days of my life, to
> gaze upon the beauty of the LORD and to seek him in his
> temple (verse 4).

There were lots of things I was asking of God that morning. But the
psalmist asked for only *one* thing: to dwell in God's presence, seeking
His face and glory.

I realized that if seeking God had been my one request—my *only*
request—I would not have needed anything else I'd been praying for:

- *If His presence had been what I sought first,* I would've had the
  confidence that He is my Provider, both financially and otherwise.

- *If His character had been all that I sought,* I would've had the
  peace of mind that He is the Great Physician for whatever my
  daughter's medical condition.

- *And if His glory had been my chief desire,* I would've had the
  perspective that He is the Healer of hurts and the Redeemer
  of all things when it came to my disappointed, restless heart.

When God becomes my Sole Desire, I am able to face whatever comes
my way. Jesus said, "Seek *first* his kingdom and his righteousness, and all
these things will be given to you as well" (Matthew 6:33).

The rest of my prayer that morning became this:

> *Simplify my heart, Lord, to have just* one *request: To* know *You*
> *and dwell with You intimately.*

Can you simplify *your* long list of requests to just one? What if *you* were to take your longing for more and turn it into a longing for more of God? Let me show you what happened when one woman did just that.

Desiring a Different Kind of More

Like Lara, Paula was also desperate for more. But in a strikingly different way.

The 42-year-old mother of three young children (and grandmother of two more children from an adult married daughter) was perfectly content with her life for a while. On staff at her large, growing church and a participant in a weekly women's Bible study, it appeared she was doing all she should do. And it appeared she had all she wanted. Until the day she realized there was so much more that she *should* be wanting.

"I came to an awful realization at a point last spring when I was studying the book of Acts that I was totally going through the motions," Paula said. "I filled in the blanks, checked the boxes, did the work, but I felt so fake. I remember thinking: *This is not it. This going-through-the-motions of filling in the blanks at Bible study is not working for me. It's becoming academic to me.*"

It was not intentional, Paula explains. She was in the right place at the right time, doing all the right things. But her *heart* wasn't in the right place.

"You can do a lot of good things and not be glorifying God in it," Paula said. When she became aware of the mechanical aspect of her relationship with God, she didn't want it to continue. In fact, it repulsed her. She cried out to God to help her be genuine in her faith and in her relationship with Him.

"It started with my desperation of telling Him, 'I just want to know You. I need *more*. More of *You*. I need to know You differently than how I know You right now.'"

Once Paula prayed that, she says, "It's been 'hold on' ever since."

The most immediate change that happened in Paula's life was that she developed a hunger for God's Word. She began to read every verse in the Bible she could find on God's love. Then she posed the question to herself: "How would your life be different now if you really believed it?" Instead of just reading a verse, she began to put the truth of it into her life and everyday situations. The result was that it transformed her life and her relationship with God.

Looking back now, Paula says, "I wasn't hungry for the Person [of Christ]. I was hungry for the knowledge [about Him]." She says that loving God and His Word more "has opened my eyes to Him in a whole new way...my faith and my passion for Him have grown in ways that I can't even explain. He has made it so clear to me that He wants me to know Him...there is such a huge difference between knowing about Him and intimately knowing Him."

Could this be the difference between being *on the edge* and standing firm in a spacious place?

Paula says there are still days when she is tempted to go out on the edge in her own way of thinking and behaving. There are still days when she could be Lara, too. But, she says, when she inserts the Word of God into her situations, and God's truth into the lies she hears from the Tempter, her life straightens out.

"I am at a point in my faith right now where I sometimes hear the lies and believe them, but it takes me a lot less time to realize I'm believing the lie," she says. "I am so passionate about God's Word and so absolutely fanatically in love with Him that He has brought me to the point where I can replace those lies so much more quickly."

The lie that we are entitled to more, apart from God, can take a woman right out to—and even over—the edge, as was seen in Lara's life. But God's Word, as seen in Paula's life, can replace those lies and bring a woman back to her spacious place where she can live solidly and be a testimony to others.

Which One Are You?

This is the ongoing tale of two women, two paths, two choices. And it's not the first time I've seen it happen. Lara is now AWOL. Many of her friends never heard from her again. Most, like me, have tried to forget about her betrayal and move on.

But Paula? She continues to be a blessing in other women's lives while working on staff at her church, as well as when she mentors women one-on-one. She is also taking time to train her children in the relationship—not the routine—of knowing and loving God.

Consider the two scenarios: two real-life women who each had a choice and each had two paths set out before them. One woman was desperate for more of *everything*. The other was desperate for more of *God*.

One woman alienated most of those who knew her and lives today on a smaller scale, one in which she is the central figure in the drama of her life. The other woman glorifies God with all that she is and is a blessing to all who come in contact with her. Paula—the woman who wanted more of God—sees her life as all about the One who *gave* her life. And she continues, daily, to give her life back to Him.

Which woman will *you* be? And what path will *you* take?

God told His people centuries ago that He had set two paths before them—two paths that are before us, too, as women on the edge:

> See, I set before you today life and prosperity, death and destruction. For I command you today to love the LORD your God, to walk in his ways, and to keep his commands, decrees and laws; then you will live and increase, and the LORD your God will bless you…But if your heart turns away and you are not obedient, and if you are drawn away to bow down to other gods [our own desires; the world's expectations; our lust for money, love, or power] and worship them, I declare to you this day that you will certainly be destroyed…This day I call heaven and earth as witnesses against you that I have set before you life and death, blessings and curses. *Now choose life*, so that you and your children may live and that you may love the LORD your God, listen to his voice, and hold fast to him. For the LORD is your life…(Deuteronomy 30:15-20).

I love how God doesn't just set the choice before us and walk away, leaving us to decide our own destiny. He instead *pleads* with His people to choose the right path to their destiny: "Now *choose* life…for the LORD is your life…"

The Choice Is Yours

When Eve was tempted to want more, she had two paths in front of her. She could choose the knowledge of evil (death and destruction) or she could choose the fruit of the tree of life. Oh, if only she had chosen life! Instead, she chose *knowledge* over life. She chose to know of more than she, in her innocence, knew. She wanted *more* in her life, and ended up losing her life because of it.

David, the psalmist, a man who met many crossroads throughout his life, recognized that God was the One who laid the paths before him. And God never made the right path a mystery. "You have made known to me the path of life," David sang in Psalm 16:11. "You will fill me with joy in your presence, with eternal pleasures at your right hand."

And in Isaiah 30:21 we read that God is, again, faithful in letting us know which path to take: "Whether you turn to the right or to the left, your ears will hear a voice behind you, saying 'This is the way; walk in it.'"

Oh, I want to hear that whisper behind me, don't you? And I want to obey it and find joy in God's presence, and eternal pleasures at His right hand.

Think about it, my friend. Does God really need to *plead* with you to choose life? Isn't the answer obvious? Aren't the benefits (life and blessings) apparent?

Which path will you take? Will you allow your desperation for more to lead you down a path toward destruction? Or will you channel that desire for more into a desire for *more of God* and let Him lead you toward a destiny of delight?

I know which path I want to take. How about *you*?

Finding Your Spacious Place

He brought me out into a spacious place; he
rescued me because He delighted in me.

PSALM 18:19

We are women on the edge when we continue to want more in spite of our blessings. Yet when we are content, we have found our spacious place—the place where we are no longer living on the edge, but living fully in God's purpose for us. If Eve had cherished her oneness with God, and trusted Him with all He had given—and what He chose *not* to give—she never would've felt He was withholding something from her. If she had learned to be content with the Lover of her soul, she never would have listened to the lie that she needed more than she already had. If she had embraced her spacious place in paradise, she never would've had to leave.

Work through the following exercises this week to help you find that spacious place of contentment when you begin to feel you want or need something more.

1. Make a list of the things that come to mind when you consider what *more* you wish you had:

2. Now list the blessings in your life:

I recently came across the following statistics, which shocked and convicted me about my heart that so often longs for more:

> If you have food in your refrigerator, clothes on your back, a roof overhead and a place to sleep, you are richer than 75 percent of the people in this world. If you have *any* money in the bank and some in your wallet and some spare change in a dish somewhere, you are among the top 8 percent of the world's wealthy; 92 percent have less to live on than you do! If you have never experienced the danger of battle, the loneliness of imprisonment, the agony of torture, or the pangs of starvation, you are ahead of 500 million other people in the world. If you can attend worship services at church without the fear of harassment, arrest, torture, or death, you are more blessed than three billion people in the world.[2]

3. Write out a prayerful response to the paragraph above.

4. Read Psalm 27:4. If you, like David, boiled all your desires down to "one thing," what would that be?

5. Using Psalm 27:4 as a guide, write out your prayer to the Lord, telling Him the *one thing* you desire in a way that puts Him first.

2

Desperate for Control

DESIRING A SURRENDERED HEART

You're blessed when you feel you've lost what
is most dear to you. Only then can you be
embraced by the One most dear to you.

MATTHEW 5:4 MSG

For the sake of your name lead and guide me.
Free me from the trap that is set for me,
for you are my refuge.

PSALM 31:3-4

What is it about *not* being in control that makes us women on the edge?

Listen, for yourself, to the cries of a few women desperate to take matters into their own hands:

Joyce, who was married to Jim for 37 years, found herself struggling in her first year as a widow:

> I am doing well coming from the valley of grief, but the issues of loneliness and learning to do life alone is my present challenge. I am having some difficulty trusting the Lord that what life is like today won't be this way forever.
>
> A recent car accident put me into another difficult situation of dealing with things by myself. The woman who rear-ended my car has a small insurance company that has been dragging its heels about getting my car repaired. The accident happened three weeks ago this past Monday, and my car is still sitting

in the body shop waiting for her insurance to go through the paperwork and process to get the bumper replaced. A bumper! I am thankful that God protected me from injury and my car was not damaged seriously, but we are approaching a month and it still has not been repaired!

If only Joyce could be in control of the timing and get this situation taken care of!

Adriana, 48 years old and still single, *knows* God is in control of the intimate details of her life. And yet...

It never used to bother me that I had not met the "man of my dreams," but now as I've gotten older and the lines on my face have crept in, I have found myself thinking about it more. I've wondered if I'm on the right path, whether there is someone for me out there or not. There are times when I feel life is passing me by. And I wonder if God has forgotten.

If Adriana had her way, the man of her dreams would have been in her life long ago.

Janet's inability to control her husband's addiction leaves her wondering if there's any hope for change:

I have been married 38 years to the same man but with two different personalities. I say that because during the last 20 years he has been a compulsive gambler. We have both, at different times, been seeking help to understand and control this situation. I have no idea why, after so many years, he started this behavior. I have to understand that it is an addiction or disease like alcohol and drugs. It has cost us several thousands of dollars and most of my retirement fund. Now that we are in our sixties, this is extremely scary for me! I have lost all trust in him. I am suspicious of everything he

says. Months go by sometimes with no new "events." Then
I begin to forgive and let my guard down, and it all starts
over again. Some say to put him out on his own and let him
"hit bottom." Others say that is not the Christian thing to
do because it is an illness like cancer. I wonder what I did
to deserve this. Why is he lying to me all the time? He says
he loves me, and I love him. Sometimes I just feel alone and
ready to jump off a cliff!

If Janet could change her husband's ways, she would. But she can't.
So where is God in all of this?

We read in the Bible that Sarah was 65 years old when God promised her husband, Abraham, that he would have a son. But God didn't
seem to be in as much of a hurry as Sarah was. As she continued to grow
older and God continued to delay, she finally decided—about ten years
into the waiting—that she had waited long enough. She may have had
thoughts along these lines:

> If we're going to have a baby anytime soon, I'm apparently
> going to have to take charge and make it happen. I'll give my
> maid, Hagar, to my husband, and when she conceives and
> bears a child, it will be mine. That must be how my husband
> and I will receive our long-awaited heir.

Sarah's plan backfired, however. The results were disastrous. About
15 years later, she finally had a son, Isaac, born of her own body. But
because she tried to take the matter into her own hands, she caused the
birth of Ishmael and a people who would oppose her own son's people all
through the rest of history. Sarah sacrificed her intimacy with her husband and her trust in God, and complicated her son's future, all because
she couldn't wait for *God's* plan to come to fruition—a plan that was
much better than hers.[3]

Chalk It Up to the Curse

Why is the longing for control so very powerful in a woman's life?

What is at the source of this compulsion that makes us women on the edge? I believe the answer lies in how we were made…or rather, what we've made of ourselves.

In the creation story in the Bible, we're told that God created man and woman in His own likeness. We were made in *His* image, with *His* characteristics.[4] That means we were created with the ability to administrate, oversee, manage. Eve, the first woman, was commanded to rule creation alongside her husband. But after Eve decided she wanted more than was given her (as we saw in chapter 1), her punishment consisted of being cursed with an unquenchable desire to control.

When God punished Eve for her disobedience, He not only increased the pain she would experience in bearing children, but He put her in the position of "desiring" her husband's authority. God said, "Your desire will be for your husband, and he will rule over you" (Genesis 3:16). Eve's resulting "desire" for her husband wouldn't be a sexual desire. Nor would it be an emotional longing for his love and attention. The word "desire" in that verse refers to an unhealthy desire that could bring about destructive results.[5] When God told Eve that she would "desire" her husband, He was saying she would covet his control, seek the position of authority that he was given. Her desire, or drive, would be to have the authority in the relationship. And that desire to control—that blinding obsession to get out from under male authority and have things *our* way—has been a source of frustration and edginess for women ever since.

How natural it is for us, then, to want to administrate—to the point that *we* are the ones in charge. Naturally, we want our home, job, finances, relationships, and so on to be under control, working harmoniously, bringing us joy. We want that so much that it drives us to the edge, at times, when aspects of our life seem out of control. Now that we are living in a sin-stained world, life this side of heaven will never be perfect, complete, thoroughly under control, and harmonious. Therefore, our desire to create and manage and administrate (God's likeness in us) is distorted. It results in our wanting to be "god" in our own little worlds.

There are certain things I think I can do better than my husband. And this annoys him. He isn't annoyed by the fact that I can do them better (actually, that "fact" is still under debate!), but it bugs him when I insist on "helping" him with something by "suggesting" a better way to do something, or when I just forge ahead and do certain things on my own, assuming he would've preferred my method anyway. In fact, Hugh once admitted to me that he's convinced that often when I ask for his advice, I am merely looking for agreement with my own plans so I can move ahead with what I have already decided to do. Ouch! Is my controlling nature *that* evident?

In reality, I am not as good of an administrator as I believe myself to be. In fact, there are times I make a pretty good mess of things. And I believe when that happens, there are lessons God wants me to learn so I will gladly hand back to Him the reins of control and admit that I make a lousy god. And yet, when I think about it, why wouldn't I want God to have the reins in the first place?

God's Ability to Govern

When Job (whose story is told in the Bible) lost everything he had—his physical possessions, his investments, his livelihood, his ten children, his dignity, and his health—and he could do nothing about his circumstances, he reached a place of freedom, rather than frustration, at which he was able to declare to God:

> I know that you can do all things; no plan of yours can be thwarted (Job 42:1).

Throughout the Bible, God reassures us He has a plan for our lives and He is in control of it, regardless of how things might look. The psalmists sang it, the Old Testament prophets declared it, and the New Testament writers confirmed it: God is the One who is in control.

God Is in Control of Our Safety and Protection

We can invest in a top-of-the-line security system for our homes and take all sorts of precautionary measures to protect everything that we have, but ultimately God is the One who protects us and keeps us safe. The psalmists tell us:

> I will lie down and sleep in peace, for you alone, O LORD, make me dwell in safety (Psalm 4:8).

> My help comes from the LORD, the Maker of heaven and earth. He will not let your foot slip—he who watches over you will not slumber (Psalm 121:2-3).

God Is in Control of Our Destiny

We can plan out our lives, but ultimately God is in control of our destiny. Scripture tells us He knows the end of our days and has assigned us our "portion" and established our "delightful inheritance":

> LORD, you have assigned me my portion and my cup; you have made my lot secure. The boundary lines have fallen for me in pleasant places; surely I have a delightful inheritance. I will praise the LORD, who counsels me...Because he is at my right hand, I will not be shaken (Psalm 16:5-8).

> "For I know the plans I have for you," declares the LORD, "plans to prosper you and not to harm you, plans to give you hope and a future" (Jeremiah 29:11).

God Is in Control Regardless of How Fearful Our Situation Looks

We sometimes look at our circumstances and think God is not there, or we think He is unaware of our situation and that we need to step in and control things ourselves. But Scripture assures us God is ever aware and ever in charge:

> The LORD is my light and my salvation—whom shall I fear? The LORD is the stronghold of my life—of whom shall I be afraid? (Psalm 27:1-2).

> God is our refuge and strength, an ever-present help in trouble. Therefore we will not fear, though the earth give way and the mountains fall into the heart of the sea, though its waters roar and foam and the mountains quake with their surging (Psalm 46:1-3).

> When you pass through the waters, I will be with you; and when you pass through the rivers, they will not sweep over you. When you walk through the fire, you will not be burned; the flames will not set you ablaze (Isaiah 43:2).

God Is in Control Even When It Looks Like We've Made a Mess of Things

God is so gracious that even when we start trying to control things and we mess up, He steps in and gets us back on the right path:

If the LORD delights in a man's way, he makes his steps firm; though he stumble, he will not fall, for the LORD upholds him with his hand (Psalm 37:23-24).

We know that in all things God works for the good of those who love him, who have been called according to his purpose (Romans 8:28).

God Is in Control Even When We Think We Are the Ones in Control

There are times we just plain forget about God. We forge ahead with our own plan and truly believe we are the ones who will make it happen. But that doesn't lessen God's role or ability to control all things:

It was not by their sword that they won the land, nor did their arm bring them victory; it was your right hand, your arm, and the light of your face, for you loved them (Psalm 44:3).

Do you have an arm like God's, and can your voice thunder like his? Then adorn yourself with glory and splendor, and clothe yourself in honor and majesty. Unleash the fury of your wrath, look at every proud man and bring him low…crush the wicked where they stand…Then I myself will admit to you that your own right hand can save you (Job 40:9-12,14).

God Is in Control of All that Occurs in the Universe

We agree God controls the earth's orbit and holds the galaxies in place. Yet if He has those things under control, can't He also control the events of our life, which are miniscule in comparison? In fact, that's the question God asked of Job, a mere man who thought he understood God's ways:

Have you ever given orders to the morning, or shown the dawn its place…? …Have you journeyed to the springs of the sea or walked in the recesses of the deep? …Have you comprehended the vast expanses of the earth? Tell me, if you know all this (Job 38:12,16,18).

And the psalmists repeatedly declared that God is able to do things we can't even fathom:

The Mighty One, God, the LORD, speaks and summons the earth from the rising of the sun to the place where it sets (Psalm 50:1).

God Is in Control of Our Personal Provision

Again, if God can control the vast complexities of the universe, He can control the circumstances and events in our lives to provide us what we need:

You care for the land and water it; you enrich it abundantly. The streams of God are filled with water to provide the people with grain, for so you have ordained it (Psalm 65:9).

My God will meet all your needs according to his glorious riches in Christ Jesus (Philippians 4:19).

And Jesus Himself told us that just as our heavenly Father provides food for the birds of the air and clothes for the lilies of the field, so will He provide for our needs as well:

Do not worry about your life, what you will eat or drink or about your body, what you will wear...Look at the birds of the air; they do not sow or reap or store away in barns, and yet your heavenly Father feeds them. Are you not much more valuable than they? (Matthew 6:25-26).

That sounds like a pretty clear "Don't worry about it" statement from the Son of God, doesn't it? In other words, "You have a God who is in control; so don't you feel *you* have to be!"

When We Get in the Way

Not only is God perfectly able to control all the events of our lives (remember that He sees the future, near and far, and we don't), but He is good and loving and incapable of making a mistake. That means all He has not yet done is for a good reason. And all He is yet to do is bound to be spectacular.

Yet we still want things *our* way and we want them *now*. We still desire control, not realizing that when we are in control (or at least when we think we are), we are in a sense saying, "God, you're not running things as well as I can. Move aside."

Jesus declared God's tremendous ability to control our lives when He told us in John 15:5, "Apart from me you can do nothing." He was basically saying that—try as we may—God is the One who accomplishes things in our lives, and without Him we are powerless. Some people look at the flip side of that verse, rejoicing that with God's help we can accomplish anything. But on days when I am tempted to try to take control of a situation, I have to remember Jesus' actual words: "Apart from me you can do *nothing*." When I take steps to control a situation, I am edging God out and attempting to speed things up on my own or accomplish something without Him. Do you ever do that, too? Let's face it—God is God. He doesn't need our help with anything. So either we let Him be in charge and do what He does best, or we try to take charge and fail miserably.

We are also told in the Bible that if we are trusting Christ Jesus for our salvation that we are "chosen, having been predestined according to the plan of him *who works out everything in conformity with the purpose of his will*" (Ephesians 1:11). Our efforts to control anything apart from God's purposes will surely fail.

In fact, the only thing we are commanded in Scripture to control is our own behavior. In First Thessalonians 4:3-4 we are told, "It is God's will that you should be sanctified: that you should avoid sexual immorality; that *each of you should learn to control his own body* in a way that is holy and honorable."

God doesn't want us to try to control the situations that are clearly in His realm and His responsibility. He wants us to trust in His character and His Word and leave the reins to Him. However, He does expect us to exert self-discipline over certain matters that are clearly *within* our ability to control. My friend, Jenny, learned this lesson in a rather dramatic way.

Our Plans versus God's Plans

Jenny pretty much believed she was in control of her life...until God turned it upside down and showed her who was *really i*n charge.

I met Jenny when I spoke at a military base in Fairbanks, Alaska. A beautiful and gracious hostess, she had about 20 women in her living room for dinner the night before I spoke at a women's conference near the base. Family pictures lined the walls of her beautiful home. I remember thinking, *What a beautiful woman, and so proud of her family.*

But Jenny told me at the conference the next day that for years she didn't feel her family was complete.

"I was desperate for a fifth child," she said. "I was obsessed with the idea of completing our family." When she finally became pregnant with her fifth child, she suffered a miscarriage that hospitalized her and had her on bed rest for almost a month.

"The loss of a baby was devastating," she said. "But I had *my* plans: heal for three months, get pregnant in June, my husband would deploy in September, and all would be 'back on track.'"

God had a different plan, however. The first Sunday in May, Jenny's husband, Bill, woke up not feeling well.

"I took our four kids and went to church. By the time we got home, Bill was having such horrible pain that I took him to the hospital emergency room. After six hours and multiple tests, we were sent home with the news that he had a tumor on his pancreas.

"On the drive home, I looked at him and, with his chin quivering, he simply said, 'I won't be around to give away my girls at their weddings.'"

The following day, Bill had an MRI and doctors decided the tumor needed to come out right away. So they scheduled surgery in Washington State (because Bill and Jenny's home state of Alaska did not have the resources to do the surgery). Their doctor sent the MRI results away for a second opinion. Jenny said, "For three full days, we believed that Bill had pancreatic cancer, and had only six months to live.

"Once again, I began making *my* plans: check on the insurance policy, decide where I would raise our four children, and so on. And, once again, God had other plans."

Jenny and Bill later received a call that the MRI had been incorrectly read. The tumor was pushing up *against* the pancreas, not coming *from* it. The next logical conclusion was that Bill had lymphoma. They learned that would involve surgery, chemotherapy, and possibly radiation for the purpose of buying time.

"Basically, they were trying to get the cancer into remission," Jenny said. "During this time, the doctors said that if we wanted to take a vacation, the middle two weeks of June was the best time.

"Our lives were about to change dramatically—either from surgery and all that it would entail, or just from the ongoing chemo and radiation that Bill was facing," Jenny said. For two months, as Bill had tests run, blood drawn, and they awaited results, Jenny realized maybe it was time for her to stop planning and turn everything over to God.

"During this time of waiting, I was on a walk when I was hit with the obvious. I was trying to plan the future, control things I couldn't control, and was laying down my 'burdens' at Jesus' feet. It was as if I had made a to-do list. On *my* list was plan the future; and on God's list I had placed the 'burdens' I don't like to deal with—weight loss, my finances, and so on. This was the time when I let go (as if I ever had control of anything), took hold of my responsibility for the things I *could* control, and let God take over the rest."

As part of letting go and trusting God with what was out of their control, Bill and Jenny took a family trip to Europe—a trip they believed might be their last vacation together.

"Upon returning from Europe, we received a wonderful phone call. The diagnosis was that Bill had a highly curable testicular cancer," Jenny said. "After undergoing four months of intense chemotherapy, Bill was completely healed."

In retrospect, Jenny looks at all that happened and recounts her blessings rather than hold on to any bitterness. In light of Bill's treatments, the doctors don't know if Bill and Jenny will ever be able to have a fifth child. But rather than mourning that as a loss, Jenny is praising God that her husband is still alive.

"If I had been given this news [of not being able to have a fifth child] back in March, after the miscarriage, I would have been devastated. After the experience of this past year, I thank God for my four children and the wonderful husband He's allowed me to *keep.*"

Jenny also cites, as blessings, an "amazing trip" to Europe that God allowed them to experience as a family, and the fact that their journey through cancer has greatly increased their realm of ministry. "Now we can minister and relate to such a wider spectrum of needs," she said.

One verse that constantly came to Jenny's mind as she was attempting to control her situation was Jeremiah 29:11: "'I know the plans I have for you,' declares the LORD, 'plans to prosper you and not to harm you, plans to give you hope and a future.'"

"In the past, my optimistic mind had put the emphasis on 'plans to prosper you' (woo hoo!). Now, suddenly it became clear that the emphasis for *me* had to be God saying. '*I* know the plans *I* have for you.' It was okay for me to not know or control. I had to let go and let *God* be in control."

Jenny also found comfort, and conviction, in Psalm 46:10: "Be still, and know that I am God."

"As an Army wife, homeschooling mom, church musician, and so on, the 'be still' part of that verse was what always spoke to me. Now suddenly, in the light of my world collapsing, the verse spoke differently to me. It was suddenly, 'Be still and know that *I am God!*' I was expending so much energy trying to plan, control, and just do something to fix my world that I needed a reminder that the God of the universe loved me and had a perfect plan for my life. Yes, I had the peace that surpasses all understanding, and I could quote verse after verse about God being in control. But until your world is rocked by something this drastic, *knowing* God's peace and *experiencing* His peace are two very different things."

Surrendering Control

Looking back on her season of surrendering control to God, Jenny says she kept trying to give God the areas of her life that she wanted changed—particularly weight loss and financial responsibility. God gave her back the areas she *could* control, and impressed upon her heart the need to give Him the rest.

"What a relief that the only thing God expected me to work on were those two areas I really *could* control—my weight and my spending. The rest—such as my husband's health and another child—really *is* out of my control."

So often we hand to God the things we don't want to take responsibility for. And ironically, we hold onto the bigger things we are powerless to change. So what are the areas we really *can* control? The list is short. In fact, there is only one thing on the list: ourselves. We can control our own attitudes and actions.

How many times do we find ourselves saying things like...

"I can't control my temper."

"I'm very emotional; I can't help it."

"I'm just a very outspoken person; I say what I feel and I can't help it."

"I've always been this way, and it will probably never change."

"I've been smoking for forty years. I've tried to stop and I can't."

"I'm [insert your nationality here] and we're just that way. It's in our blood."

Those are excuses. In fact, I'll go so far as to say they are lies. God's Word holds us accountable for our actions, so none of those excuses are valid. God's Word tells us to control...

- our behavior and lifestyle (Romans 12:1; Galatians 5:16)
- our temper (Ephesians 4:26-27)
- our speech (Ephesians 4:29)
- our thoughts (Philippians 4:8)

We live in a society that labels our lack of control an addiction. We can be addicted to alcohol, drugs, smoking, sex, pornography, food, gambling, shopping, eating, working, and even exercising. Anything we do or even *think about* in excess is an addiction. However, we are still commanded by God to control our addictions.[6]

If you struggle with controlling yourself in an area that you believe may be an addiction, I encourage you to seek the help and accountability of organizations that specialize in helping people overcome their addictions. My Dad, who is more than 25 years sober from his addiction to alcoholism, is living proof that organizations like Overcomers Outreach[7] can help a person, in the power of Jesus Christ, to overcome their addictions. However, I want to remind you that if you have Christ living within you, you have the power to overcome anything. Scripture tells us, "I can do everything through him who gives me strength" (Philippians 4:13). And that "incomparably great power" that raised Jesus from the dead is the same power that is at work in your life to help you overcome weaknesses or addictions (Ephesians 1:18-20).

In short, you and I, through the power of Christ, can control our *own* behavior, but not the circumstances that are thrust upon us. We can control our *own* thoughts, moods, and actions, but not the thoughts, moods, and actions of others.

What's Eating at *You*?

Much of what we want, we want immediately. Yet if God hasn't delivered, there's a reason for that. If He has not fulfilled your request, then either His answer is no or wait. Sometimes it's difficult for us to distinguish between the two. In some cases it's possible God wants to teach us something while we're in the waiting room. Among the things He wants to teach us are a confidence in His character, a trust in His Word, and an unswerving dependence on Him. As we persevere through a frustrating situation, we are forced to rely on Him and admit that He is in control. That humbles us. That reminds us that He is God and we are not. And that makes us women who *revere* God rather than try to *be* God.

Stories of Surrender

At the beginning of this chapter, I mentioned some women who were desperate to control their situations. Eventually they realized that their lack of control—and learning to be okay with it—was part of the lesson and the blessing God wanted to give them in their state of frustration.

Joyce—the new widow whose damaged car sat unrepaired in a shop—saw God in her circumstance, even though He wasn't working according to the timing she had hoped.

While still frustrated with her situation, she was able to say, "I have learned and progressed through many simple 'exercises,' but I was not prepared to deal with this kind of thing alone. I may not see the reasoning in having to wait, but He does, and He has a lesson for me in the process. I am struggling, but He knows what lies ahead and I don't. There may be a good reason it's better for my car to sit in the body shop rather than for me to drive it right now. It may not make sense to me, but for some reason God sees that as a good thing."

Today, Joyce looks back on that situation with the assurance that God really was in control of all that was happening.

"Something about lacking any control over the direction life takes us gives us a true perspective of reality," Joyce said. She not only learned to surrender to God during that frustrating time, but she became convinced that He had a plan all along. Joyce's minor accident brought to her attention several details that needed to be changed in her insurance policy now that she was a widow. For instance, she needed a lower deductible (since she no longer had both her and her husband's income to pay the deductible in the case of an accident). And she added a rental car benefit to her policy now that she had only her car, and not her husband's as well. With those policy changes, she realized she could afford to pay a bit more for the policy each month than the huge out-of-pocket expenses she was facing from the small accident that had just occurred.

"As soon as I made the changes on my insurance policy, the collision center called to tell me they had received the check for the repair. Driving home, I realized had it not been for this minor accident, I would not have thought about the importance of changing my insurance policy to fit my needs [as a widow]. God had been in control of the situation and was allowing the delays to guide me."

Today, Joyce faces her future more confidently, knowing God truly is in control and she is not alone.

"Another year has passed since my husband's death," Joyce said. "Life still hands out difficulties and the doubts and fears still try to seep in and drown my faith that God has everything under control. When I get tired or frustrated, the sadness and loneliness returns, but it is temporary. I trust what God has written in His Word and the things He has proven to me in the midst of difficulties."

Adriana, the 48-year-old single woman awaiting the man of her dreams, realizes that the One who created her hasn't forgotten about her after all.

"I take hope in Isaiah 25:1: 'In perfect faithfulness you have done marvelous things, things planned long ago.'

"Even though it seems likes He's taking forever, He has a plan," Adriana said. "He knows. It's already been done. It's getting to be time to walk into that moment in time."

Psalm 13 is often the prayer of Adriana's heart:

How long, O LORD? Will you forget me forever?
How long will you hide your face from me?

> How long must I wrestle with my thoughts
>> And every day have sorrow in my heart? (verses 1-2).

"It's difficult when we see so many loose ends that we want to see tied up—whether it's finding the man of our dreams, landing that perfect job, or waiting for our family members to come to a saving knowledge of Christ—and we say 'Lord, I've been faithful, I haven't sidetracked and I'm hoping You're going to get me to that place I want to be,' and yet God can be silent many times."

But, she says, the key is believing. "We have such trouble believing… we have trouble believing because we're thinking 'Why me?' and 'How will this really happen?'"

Yet Adriana wants her song to be that of the psalmist at the *end* of Psalm 13:

> I trust in your unfailing love;
>> My heart rejoices in your salvation.
> I will sing to the LORD,
>> for he has been good to me (verses 5-6).

Adriana's song does sound similar to the psalmist's.

"There is such joy that comes in surrender," she said, "surrendering control to God—as if we ever had any—and saying, "I know *Your* will is better than mine.""

And Janet, who was so frustrated with her husband's gambling addiction that she wanted to jump off a cliff, did find a light at the end of the tunnel:

> For several months now, my husband and I have had coun-
> seling from pastors and therapists. We are learning to com-
> municate better. A lot of what was happening between us
> was because of his inability to express his feelings and my
> anger issues. We still have a lot of financial problems, but then
> who doesn't in the current economy? He was in a really bad
> car accident last month and the car was totaled. He is going
> through extensive therapy for back and neck injuries and is

in a lot of pain. Right now I am trusting God to handle our situations. I truly believe that God wants us to work through all of this and stay together.

Now there's a woman who once seemed without hope, but has since realized—through not being able to control her circumstances—that God truly *is* working in their midst and He does have a plan and a future for her and her husband.

Did you notice a common thread running through each of those stories? Each woman went from being desperate to *get* to being desperate for *God*. Instead of continuing to seek a result or a prize, they began to seek God as their prize. They surrendered their desire for control and found, in place of it, a desire for the One who is in control. And they are now resting in Him.

Proverbs 16:3 says, "Commit to the LORD whatever you do, and your plans will succeed." Commit, it says, which implies yielding or handing over the matter to God's wisdom and direction.

Joyce had to commit to God the situation with her car, and He worked everything out. Adriana had to yield her hopes and dreams for a husband to God, and she continues to trust Him to meet the longings of her heart, whether it be through Himself or with a person He chooses to bring into her life. Janet had to commit to God her husband's gambling addiction, and God appears to be shining the light on their path.

God's Name Is on the Line

When we surrender the reins to God, we are letting Him show us that He is God. We are giving Him a chance to back up His Word and protect His name. That's right—God has a reputation to keep when it comes to keeping His eye on us. The psalmist prayed in Psalm 31:3, "You are my rock and my fortress, *for the sake of your name* lead and guide me."

In her book *When Life and Beliefs Collide*, Carolyn Custis James says, "God's glory is bound up with his reputation, his great name, his honor. God's reputation can never be divorced from what happens to us." Carolyn then goes on to quote Bible teacher and author John Piper: "It was God's good pleasure to join you to Himself in such a way that His name is at stake in your destiny—in such a way that what becomes of you reflects upon His name."[8]

Isn't it wonderfully comforting to know that how God manages our affairs—how He chooses to control our lives—reflects on His reputation for being a good, kind, loving, and faithful God? That assures me that He will be true to His Word and character and He will glorify Himself in how He manages my life—and yours.

So, my friend, if your failed attempts to control life have you on the edge, find your spacious place by resting in the only One who can control all that you cannot. And pretty soon your desire will not be for the control, but for the One who is ultimately *in* control.

Finding Your Spacious Place

I have set the LORD always before me.
Because he is at my right hand, I will not be shaken.
PSALM 16:8

Our desire to be in control leads us out to the edge. But surrendering to the One who controls all things with His loving, capable hands helps us stay in a spacious place where we let Him control our lives and we reap the benefits. Surrender your heart to Him by working through the following steps:

1. List here the situations or circumstances that you've been wanting God to control that *you* are actually responsible for:

2. What situations are truly outside of your control that you must surrender to God?

3. Read the following verses of Scripture and write them out below. Then personalize each one to apply to your particular situation (I have done the first one for you):

   Romans 8:28: "We know that in all things God works for the good of those who love him, who have been called according to his purpose."

   My personal application: I know that God will use this unexpected financial situation for good in my life, perhaps to teach me a deeper trust in His provision.

James 1:2-3:

My personal application:

Jeremiah 29:11:

My personal application:

Psalm 25:15:

My personal application:

Ephesians 3:20:

My personal application:

4. Reread pages 33–36. Which of God's abilities to govern is particularly comforting to you?

Pick one of the verses in that section to memorize and write it out here:

5. Ask God to replace your desire to control with a desire for the One who is *in* control. Read the following prayer, fill in the blank as it best applies to you, and sign and date the bottom as a reminder to yourself of the commitment you have made to Him:

> Lord Jesus, You are the only One truly capable of controlling _____, which is distressing my heart right now. I surrender to you my insistence on trying to work this out myself, and I place my trust in Your control over this situation and Your promise to see me through it. Thank You for Your ability to do immeasurably more than I can ask or imagine according to Your power that is at work within me. I rest in You and Your care.
>
> Your Servant: _____
>
> Date: _____

3

Desperate for Fulfillment

DESIRING A GRATEFUL HEART

Thou hast made us for thyself, O Lord; and
our heart is restless until it rests in thee.

ST. AUGUSTINE

All my longings lie open before you, O Lord;
My sighing is not hidden from you.

PSALM 38:9

A women's magazine I received in the mail this morning told me,
once more, that I could have it all.

How to Get More Out of Life: Simple Steps to...

- good lovin'
- rock-solid confidence
- the perfect outfit
- more time for you
- and *everything else* you really want!

Wow...if only it were that easy. If only we could read a four-page
magazine article and find *everything else* we really want. If only that's
what it took to feel completely fulfilled. But after celebrities share their
formulas for finding self-worth, men offer women advice on how to be the
ultimate catch, and psychologists reveal remedies (like eating chocolate
and having a sexual fling) that are believed to make women feel better
about themselves, we end up feeling empty again.

The fact that such headlines sell so many women's magazines speaks volumes about the longings of women today. We are hoping for happiness, searching for self-worth, trying to be someone we aren't. We are unfulfilled. And we are on the edge.

Over the past year alone, more than 100 women of all ages and walks of life have answered for me this question: What have you really wanted that God has withheld from you?

The answers reveal what many women are searching for in hopes of fulfillment:

- "I'm still waiting to find the man of my dreams."

- "My greatest desire is to have a baby."

- "I am desperate to have a relationship with my adult children."

- "I often feel that if my father would just love me, my life would be complete."

- "I'm waiting for acceptance and approval from my family."

- "I want to experience the joy of being 'equally yoked' with a godly husband."

- "My greatest desire is to have family unity and peace in my home."

- "For God to open the doors of ministry and reveal to me what I was called to do."

- "I've always wanted to _____" (answers included play the piano, write a book, have a singing career).

Some women, however, were looking for the unattainable:

- "I want to be financially secure enough to write a tithe check without a backward glance or wondering if there will be enough to pay the rest of my bills." (As if *any* of us ever get to that place!)

- "I've always wanted the 'perfect Christian family.'" (As if *any* of us are!)

- "I long to have the ideal husband and the perfect marriage." (As if such were even possible!)

As you look through that list, maybe you'll find one or two that you, too, are desperate for. They are *all* good things. But are any of them enough?

Julie, a 50-year-old woman who has spent most of her life going after whatever her heart wanted, would tell you, emphatically, "No!"

Julie's Journey

I met Julie when she answered the call on my Web site to interview women who were on the edge. We met at a coffee shop and she unfolded her life story for me.

"God allowed me to go through things in life that I wouldn't wish upon any woman…things that if I had the chance to do over, I'd choose differently," Julie said.

Julie remembers being desperate for love at the age of 14. She became sexually involved with her boyfriend, and by the time she reached 16, she had an abortion to terminate an unwanted pregnancy. "I went from bad to worse through promiscuity and drugs," she said. "I still don't understand why I had so little love or concern for myself. It is by God's grace and a pure miracle that I'm alive today.

"Prior to marriage, I'd had everything that the world offered. What my heart wanted, I went after. For several years this went off and on. I'd be a normal person, and then an insatiable wandering soul."

That *insatiable wandering soul* led Julie to a miserable life as a young woman. By the time she was 19, she found herself on drugs with nowhere to live. She eventually hit rock bottom. She went home and told her mother that she felt no one really loved her except Robert, a man she was engaged to. But she was told by a counselor to wait six more months to marry him, at which time she called off the wedding. Now she wanted him back. She prayed with her mother that, if it was God's will, God would bring Robert back into her life.

One day a few years later, Julie was running late for work. She parked in a different lot than she usually did, and was allowed to leave work early. Upon returning to her car, she saw an old friend from high school who happened to know someone who still kept in contact with Robert. She tracked down his phone number, called him, made him guess who she was, and then asked "Do you ever think you could love me again?"

"He said yes, and that's the day my life changed," Julie said. She said she believes God, in His grace, led her back to Robert so she would finally feel loved by someone and get her life back on track.

Even though she married Robert a few years later and had three daughters, she didn't find herself instantly fulfilled. The insatiable longing would return now and then. But it wasn't for someone to love her anymore. It was to discover who she was and find a sense of purpose for her life. Up to this point, she had been a model, a barber at hotels and resorts, a fitness center owner, a personal trainer, a hotel concierge, an art instructor, a property management supervisor, and even a wedding photographer. "Any little thing my heart had a stirring for, I've dipped my toes into."

But it was never enough. She realizes now that all her life she sought what *she* wanted. And now she is desperate for what *God* wants of her life: "Dissatisfaction with myself, my life, and those around me has driven me to desire God in a desperate way."

Yet Julie is not turning to God as a last resort. She speaks from the place of having learned that nothing else and no one else truly satisfies. She speaks from a position of having received redemption and grace. She speaks as one who had two paths laid out before her: one that led to fulfilling her own desires, and one that led to life. She is finally able to say, "I choose *life.*"

"I've had everything, so now I am truly desperate for God. I'm desperate for *His* abundance *His* way."

Julie has now been married 27 years to Robert, and has three grown daughters and a two-year-old grandson. She has worked through many issues from her childhood and young adulthood and is rediscovering who she is in God's eyes. Julie recently took some acting and oral interpretation classes at a community college, where she had numerous opportunities to be bold in her faith toward college-aged people and encourage them not to make the mistakes she had. Recently, she auditioned for—and landed—a significant role in a stage play in which she believes she will be able to shine for God by being who He created her to be: a woman who reflects the glory of God.

Julie's desire to find self-fulfillment has turned into a desire to fulfill her Maker's purpose for her: "I'm desperate to feel His presence and do what He calls me to do. I'm ready. Desperately ready!" Her prayer today is "God, You've made me a passionate, bold, extroverted woman, and I know You have something for me...bring it on!"

"I don't want to sit in my room and let life pass me by. I don't want to stay in my pajamas anymore. I'm so ready for God to use me. I want it," she said, with tears in her eyes. "In what better place can a woman be?"

It's the *insatiable wandering soul* in all of us that leads us to do desperate things in search of fulfillment. Like a gnawing hunger that is never satisfied or a parched thirst that is never quenched, a desperate soul can never be satisfied as long as it seeks its satisfaction in the world or in its own flesh. Rachel, whose story we find in the Bible, is an example of a woman with an insatiable desire for something that would never satisfy.

Rachel's Road to Desperation

Rachel had a promising future in front of her. But she wanted children so desperately that it fractured her relationship with her sister, caused her to compromise her morals, created divisions between herself and her husband, and ultimately cost her life.

When we look at Rachel's life and trace her steps, we can see a clear road to desperation. By recognizing this road—knowing what caused her to feel so very desperate and what warning signs to look for—we can, by the grace of God, steer clear of it.

In Genesis 29, we see what began as a beautiful love story. Jacob, God's chosen heir of Abraham and Isaac, sought Rachel as his wife. But through some trickery by Rachel's father, Jacob ended up marrying Rachel's older sister, Leah. He eventually got both of the women as his wives, but he clearly loved only Rachel. Seeing that Jacob did not love Leah, God allowed Leah to conceive many children, but left Rachel barren.

Rachel's first mistake (and thus her first step down the path toward desperation) was her mind-set.

She Resented Her Circumstance

Genesis 30:1-2 says, "When Rachel saw that she was not bearing Jacob any children, she became jealous of her sister. So she said to Jacob, 'Give me children, or I'll die!' Jacob became angry with her and said, 'Am I in the place of God, who has kept you from having children?'" In Bible times, it was a cultural disgrace for women to be barren, and Rachel was probably humiliated by her infertility. The God-fearing people of the Old Testament considered conception God's providence, and often called upon the Lord to consider or bless a certain woman and open her womb.

But not once in Rachel's story do we read of her going to the Lord God and asking Him to bless her with a child. Nor do we read of her questioning God as to why she was barren. By not going to God about her infertility, we can conclude that she was not only unwilling to accept her lot, but unwilling to talk to God about it as well. Rachel wanted something she didn't have and she was determined to get it, regardless of the Lord's plans and will for her life.

Rachel's second mistake was how she chose to respond to her state of frustration.

She Responded to Her Lot in an Ungodly Way

Rachel's motives for wanting a baby weren't altogether pure. At first glance it appears that she, like many women today, just wanted a baby to hold in her arms. But Scripture makes it clear she wanted to keep up with her sister's childbearing. It's also possible she wanted in on the prestige and glory of bearing some of the sons of Israel. Regardless of her motives, however, her response to her inability to have children was jealousy toward her sister and bitterness toward her husband.

Rachel's next step of desperation came about because she was unwilling to accept God's timing.

She Rejected God's Timing and Forged Ahead with Her Own Plans

Rather than wait upon the Lord for His perfect timing, Rachel compromised her marital intimacy with Jacob and repeated a mistake of the past—she gave her maid to her husband so she could have a child through her (Genesis 30:3-8). But once was not enough. After she obtained one child that way, she gave her maid to Jacob a second time to get another child. Leah followed Rachel's example and through Leah's maid, Leah got two more sons. Rachel was still badly outnumbered in the baby department, so the duel continued.

My friend, Tom, a pastor, calls these dueling Hebrew women "Glamorous Ladies of Wrestling." His catchy sermon title for their story captures the concept well, I think. *Wrestling* is a perfect word to describe what Rachel continued to do, not only with her sister, but with her husband and God, too. In fact, in Genesis 30:8, Rachel is recorded as saying, "With mighty wrestlings I have wrestled with my sister, and I have indeed prevailed" (NASB).

Getting two children through her maid still wasn't enough, so as Rachel's obsession intensified, she resorted to superstition and bargaining.

She Resorted to Desperate Means to Get What She Wanted

Believing that mandrakes cured sterility, Rachel made use of the herbs in yet another desperate attempt to conceive a child. But she had to bargain away her husband to Leah's bed in return for the mandrakes, causing the attempt to backfire: Leah got two more sons and a daughter, while Rachel was left with nothing but useless herbs (Genesis 30:14-21).

Notice that Rachel had already tried to cheat fate (or, should we say, God's sovereignty?) by getting a child through her maid. But then she resorted to a cultural superstition believed during her day to bring about conception. With no fertility clinics around, Rachel took the next best step. But her attempts at conceiving a child were again futile.

Rachel's next mistake is shocking: When her dream for a baby was finally realized, she still was not content.

She Remained Desperate Even After Receiving What She Wanted

We would think that after finally bearing a son, Rachel would have been happy. But she wasn't. Bearing a child only served to fuel Rachel's obsession for more children. Genesis 30:22-24 says, "Then God remembered Rachel, and God gave heed to her and opened her womb. So she conceived and bore a son and said, 'God has taken away my reproach.' She named him Joseph, saying, 'May the LORD give me another son.'"[9]

One of the marks of a desperate woman is that she never really finds what she's looking for. Once Rachel received her long-awaited son, she no sooner had him cleaned off and wrapped up before she was coveting another one. Rather than relish the blessing she had just received, she was already looking for something more.

Sadly, Rachel's story closes with a dramatic end to her desperation. As she and her family were traveling, she began to suffer severe labor and gave birth to her second son. Tragically, she died as a result of childbirth.

Ironically, Rachel—who had spent most of her life longing for children—died while fulfilling that desperate wish. And a woman who expected children, rather than the Lord, to bring her joy spent her last breath giving her newborn son a name that means "the son of my sorrow" or "child of my grief."[10] Ultimately her heart's greatest desire brought about her grief and demise.

It's tragic that Rachel spent her married life longing for something she couldn't have, rather than allowing herself to be used by God however He wanted. She could've had a wonderful ministry as "Aunt Rachel," lovingly helping raise her sister's children. And she could've devoted herself to being a loving wife and a servant of the Lord. Instead, she focused on what she didn't have and how she could go about getting it.

The Danger of Desperation

Rachel believed if she could just have a child, she would be satisfied. But one was not enough. And one more was apparently too much for her body to bear. Desperation is dangerous because it focuses on self: what I want, what I must have, what I cannot live without. And focusing on self leads to destruction.

Jesus told us to forget ourselves and focus on a life given over to Him. "If anyone would come after me, he must deny himself and take up his cross and follow me. For whoever wants to save his life will lose it, but whoever loses his life for me will find it" (Matthew 16:25).

Jesus wasn't saying, "Give up your dreams and be miserable." He was saying, "When you give up your desires and plans and all that you think you need to be happy and are determined to just have Me, then you will truly find a life worth living." I know that's what He meant because He said in John 10:10, "The thief [Satan—who deceives us into thinking we can find fulfillment when we follow the desires of our own heart] comes only to steal and kill and destroy; I have come that they may have life, and have it to the full."

Turning It Around

Nicole's dream for fulfillment included having a husband and a home.

"All my life I've wanted a healthy partnership with a spouse who was also my best friend," Nicole says. "Even as a child, I dreamed of finding my Prince Charming and building a life with him. I've also wanted to be a homeowner—I've lived in apartments most of my life—and have my house serve as a hub of activity for family and friends."

Like Rachel, Nicole attempted to go after what she wanted, but it didn't bring her fulfillment.

"During college, I clung to the first guy who paid attention to me, even though I now recall the Lord calling me away from him. At that time, I did not have a relationship with God, and I continued to cling to this unhealthy relationship out of fear of being alone, even though I was being neglected and emotionally abused. After several years of dating, I became pregnant, and we married. This was a do-it-yourself project that failed miserably! When our daughter was two, my husband admitted to having an affair, and I was brought to my knees. I turned my life over to the Lord at that point and tried to be a godly wife, but my husband was openly opposed to my relationship with God and eventually left during our seventh year of marriage.

"While I will never regret having our beautiful daughter, I do regret not trusting God enough to walk away from this unhealthy relationship that cost me many years of pain, not to mention a lot of turmoil for our daughter. Looking back, I see why I can fully trust the Lord when He withholds something from me, even if I think it's what I want. I've learned the hard way that 'Father knows best!'"

Nicole is now in her mid-thirties and has been single for almost five years. She has gone through a spiritual recovery program as well. But, she says, "The Lord continues to withhold dating relationships from me."

A couple years ago, Nicole, along with a widow and a divorced mom from her church, began a ministry called Single Parent Fellowship (SPF) at her church.

"Although I was initially hesitant about starting it, this ministry has blessed me beyond my dreams and we are now being led and ministered to by a family pastor at our church who has taken us under his wing."

The group meets weekly for prayer, parenting book discussions, Bible reading, and fellowship. They also plan activities together—they see movies, go ice skating, and take trips to the mountains. One Christmas the church bought and delivered Christmas trees to the homes of all those involved in the ministry. "We have all become extended family, and I am happier now and less alone than I was when I was married!" Nicole says. "More importantly, the Lord has forever changed my heart for single parents. He is even using me now at my workplace to encourage other young single moms in their journeys."

What caused Nicole to go from surviving to thriving as a single mom? What turned her desperation for fulfillment into a desire to serve others? She allowed God to meet her where she was. And in doing so, her desire to fulfill self developed into a desire to serve others. And *there* she has found fulfillment!

Your Road to Fulfillment

What are you still waiting for God to bring about in your life? Could His area of withholding be *your* place of ministry as well? Here are three principles that can help direct your desperation toward a delightful end so that you become a Nicole and not a Rachel…so that your story ends in delight and not destruction.

1. Realize God Knows What He's Doing in Your Life

   Although Nicole was disappointed to be divorced and desperately wanted another man in her life, she realized that she could continue to make mistakes and get into another bad relationship. So she chose to trust that God is in control, that He knows what He's doing in her life, and that His timing is far better than hers. This is where Rachel messed up. It's all about trust.

2. Reflect on What He's Already Given You

   Nicole was able to see her blessing in the midst of bitter circumstances: she had a beautiful daughter who had come out of a miserable marriage. Focusing on that blessing, she moved forward as a single mom who was going to make the best of it. This is where Rachel messed up: Instead of focusing on the fact she had a husband who loved her immensely, she kept looking at what she *didn't* have—and it drove her to desperation.

3. Redirect Your Focus Toward Others

   Instead of continuing to dwell on the fact that she was lonely and lacking, Nicole chose to be a part of a ministry that ended up not only making a difference in others' lives, but hers as well. God has a way of blessing us when we choose to bless others. Look around at other women who may be longing for the same thing you are and ask God, "How can I minister to women who are in similar circumstances?" Again, this is where Rachel missed the mark. She had a whole brood of nephews and a niece whom she could have poured her life into. She could have been Aunt Rachel into a ripe old age instead of dying young as a mother who never got to raise her children.

Eyeing the Prize

Are you still desperately seeking after something? Then, as you've seen in this chapter, you can take your desire for self-fulfillment and lay it at God's feet. He will give you a heart of gratitude for what you have and contentment in the midst of your circumstances. And He may even give you a ministry of some kind. God's Word tells us that godliness plus contentment equals great gain (1 Timothy 6:6). I call it "God's math." When we practice godliness and focus on being content, we will eventually find fulfillment.

Julie, Rachel, and Nicole were all desperately seeking *something*. Julie found out the hard way that nothing in life satisfies except for God, and fortunately she learned the lesson while she still has time to live for her Lord. Rachel only saw unfulfilled hope, even to her last dying breath. And Nicole chose to trust God with what she lacked and now she no longer notices the lack—just the blessings.

Julie and Nicole are no longer women on the edge when it comes to being desperate for fulfillment. They have, instead, found a desperation for the only One who fulfills. Will *you* find your spacious place by desperately seeking Him, too?

Finding Your Spacious Place

I called on the LORD in distress; the LORD answered
me and set me in a broad place.

PSALM 118:5 NKJV

To continue striving for anything other than God is to be a woman
on the edge. To become desperate for Him is to find your spacious place
of rest, strength, and joy.

1. Read Psalm 42:1-2. David longed for God as the deer longs for
   streams of water. What is your soul truly thirsting for?

2. What do you feel is lacking in your life?

3. What might God want to teach you by withholding it from
   you?

4. Review the three steps on the "road to fulfillment" (pages
   60-61) to see if God is leading you toward a ministry:

   • *Realize God knows what He's doing in your life*—Thank God
     for your present circumstances and surrender yourself to
     Him for His purposes.

   • *Reflect on what He's already given you*—God has given you
     resources for ministering to others. What abilities, blessings,
     and opportunities do you have right now that you wouldn't
     otherwise have if you had what you're desperate for?

- *Redirect your focus toward others*—Do you know others who long for the same thing you do, whom you can encourage or minister to by sharing your story or giving your help? How can you get closer to them so they can begin to trust you?

5. Read Psalm 139:1-6. Could a God who knows you so intimately not fulfill you, as well, with Himself? Write your prayerful response to those verses in the space below.

4

Desperate for Change

DESIRING A DEEPER TRUST

How long must I wrestle with my thoughts
and every day have sorrow in my heart?

PSALM 13:2

My soul is in anguish.
How long, LORD, how long?

PSALM 6:3

Kelly wrote a quick e-mail to her husband one morning. He was out of the country, and she was about to go over the edge:

A day in the life...Medical bills crashing...spent the morning embarrassing myself and begging doctors for a break. Called other doctors on behalf of a bill of Brian's...Got a letter that Zach's medical insurance doubled...Had to spend $80 on a dinner because others wouldn't kick in...Have to pay another $80 tonight for granny's birthday...Experimenting with pain meds to see if it can make a difference in my side effect...Found out I have gained 10 pounds...Got a letter from insurance that the lady I hit in the rodeo is suing me and I might need to get another lawyer besides the insurance one if she proceeds...Seems like there is a deadline of TOMORROW on these papers that I need to do something with...No one is around to help me, of course...Having a meltdown in Albertsons...

Now today...have to find someone to help me with all of

this…Doing all this stuff instead of getting ready to leave the house, work, and pack for our trip on Monday.

And you?

Pauline, too, was desperate for change. A 25-year veteran schoolteacher, she knows what it's like to experience an extremely busy year every now and then. But she's always been able to cope. This last year was different.

> I had a particularly difficult class to work with. There were many academic difficulties and several behavioral issues as well. A teaching assistant was hired for four hours a day, five days a week to assist with the class. When the assistant's husband became seriously ill she had to cut her hours back. Most weeks she helped me for only two hours instead of 20, and sometimes not at all. This left me in a very stressful place. I did not blame the assistant because her situation was beyond her control. The principal decided to keep paying her anyway to help her financially because her husband could not work. That meant there was no money to hire someone in her place.
>
> This started in September. By November I wanted to quit my job, and I was not coping at all. I was praying and trying to trust God for strength, but sometimes I think I was trying to do it alone. I felt like I was losing it and having a meltdown. I got a little bit of a break around Christmas, but by February it was all so overwhelming again. My principal did not seem to understand my situation. He tried to help in some small ways. Whenever I tried to talk to him about it, I just broke down and cried. Many times, I cried on the way to work and on the way home. I was seeing a Christian counselor and she suggested two weeks off for stress leave, but I work at a private school, which means I would have to take those two weeks without pay. I could not afford to have financial stress on top of all the other problems.
>
> By June, I was considering not returning to my job. That

was stressful as well, because teaching was all I had done for 25 years. But I knew that I could never make it through another year like that. I felt guilty knowing that, as a Christian, I should have been able to trust God more and not get so overwhelmed. I thought there was something wrong with my relationship with God.

Ingrid came home early one day and found her world turned upside down:

> I found that my husband was in full swing, watching pornography! I was totally dumbfounded. I felt frozen to the point I couldn't say a word. You can imagine how badly it hurt me. Here I was, thinking my husband was a growing Christian and that we were best friends, and he was betraying me in every sense of the word. I mean, I'm 46 years old, but I don't feel decrepit yet. To be compared to young 18-year-olds, and in such a manner, was just too much!
>
> And later, during my Internet investigation, I found out that his addiction probably went back to before I met him, which was even worse! I didn't know who he was anymore. I mean, he wasn't with another woman physically, but this newfound revelation was still harsh on my psyche! I separated from him for three weeks and felt devastated. I felt like a total failure for not knowing who he really was.

The Beauty of Brokenness

When life bombards us with troubles and we find ourselves close to—or having—a meltdown, we rake ourselves over the coals for it. *I should be able to handle this,* we tell ourselves. *What's wrong with me? Why am I falling apart over all of this?* Do we actually believe we're Superwoman? We multitask, we organize, we care for others. Then when situations make us feel like we're gonna snap, we beat ourselves up for not being able to cope. Like Kelly, Pauline, and Ingrid, we tend to think that because we have a relationship with God we should never feel like we're going to lose it. After all, God's Word says in Philippians 4:13 that "I can do *all things* through Him who strengthens me" (NASB). So, then, why do we melt down at times when our circumstances seem unbearable?

Either God was wrong when He said we could do all things through His strength in us, or we aren't *allowing* Him to strengthen us.

One thing these daring women learned is that they couldn't muster up the "Godlike strength" on their own. And they were never expected to. Neither are we.

Whoever said, "God helps those who help themselves" was wrong! As we discussed in chapter 2 about being desperate for control, God doesn't need our help. He doesn't wait for us to get going and come along and give us the final boost. He is the one who carries the entire load because we can't.

No, God doesn't help those who help themselves. God helps those who admit they *can't* help themselves!

The apostle Paul said he had a "thorn" in his flesh—something he described as "a messenger of Satan, to torment me."[11] We don't know if it was a physical defect (such as poor eyesight) or some excruciating pain that slowed him down. Some scholars believe it was a form of spiritual attack. Whatever it was, Paul thought it was given to him to keep him humble. He wrote,

> Three times I pleaded with the Lord to take it away from me. But he said to me, "My grace is sufficient for you, for my power is made perfect in weakness." Therefore I will boast all the more gladly about my weaknesses, so that Christ's power may rest on me. That is why, for Christ's sake, I delight in weaknesses, in insults, in hardships, in persecutions, in difficulties. For when I am weak, then I am strong (2 Corinthians 12:8-10).

God helps those who admit they *can't* help themselves.

When Life Turns Upside Down

Laurie can relate to a sudden shift in her life—and desperately wanting things to change—when her aging mother was diagnosed with Alzheimer's disease.

"The past few years I've experienced not only embarrassing moments but heart-wrenching, frustrating, fearful, angry, and resentful moments as well," Laurie told me. "When Mom was first diagnosed about five years ago, I thought my world had turned upside down."

Laurie's parents lived next door to her, so they were already a daily part of her life. Her Dad was almost 80 when they learned of her mother's diagnosis, so she knew the burden of her mother's care would fall on her.

Laurie was married and had three teenagers at the time. She was also working a full-time job and staying busy serving in her church. "My plate was already very full, and now I was facing this difficult challenge."

Did she desperately want out of the situation? Of course.

"One of my first reactions was fear," Laurie admitted, "fear of the unknown and fear for myself. What was going to happen to my Mom? Was she going to forget me? What if this was my destiny, too? Would my children someday have to face this same situation with me?"

But Laurie chose to trust that God was sovereignly working the situation for her benefit. She joined a support group for adult children of Alzheimer's patients and began to learn more about the disease. As a result of learning more and talking to people who were surviving or had survived this type of situation, many of her fears were eased. "I soon realized that God was going to carry us through this just like He had carried us through many other challenges," she said.

Having her parents living right next door to her was a huge blessing. They had moved there just about the time they became concerned about Laurie's mom's memory. And, Laurie's sister lived about two hours away. She was able to come often to help bear much of the burden with Laurie.

In addition to the logistics, Laurie has seen God work in the situation in other ways. "Alzheimer's is a horrific disease and has many devastating affects on both the patient and the family. Often patients become strong-willed and difficult to deal with. While we've faced many challenges, for the most part my Mom has been very compliant and easygoing; quite unlike her 'normal' personality!

"My Mom and I were never very close, and our relationship had its difficulties. I was saddened that we had never really enjoyed each other, and I always felt that I was missing something by not having an intimate mother-daughter relationship with her. At first I was resentful that

I was having to be her caregiver when I felt she wasn't the caring Mom I needed as a child. My Mom was not a "Christian" mother like I longed for (even though she's always claimed to be a Christian). She never taught me spiritual things or took me to church. I was saved when I was about twelve and never had the chance to share spiritual things with her. She pretty much thought I was a religious fanatic! I had always hoped that she would have some sort of spiritual renewal and finally receive Christ as her personal Savior, and that we would somehow have this fantastic relationship. When I saw her slipping away from reality I realized that hope was slipping away too. I was angry. But even though Mom and I may never have the spiritual discussions I longed for, we have culti-vated a more intimate relationship and much healing has taken place in my heart."

God apparently knew what He was doing by putting Laurie in the situation she was in. He was mending a mother-daughter relationship in a way that nothing else could have.

"I've got to tell you, God is GOOD!" Laurie says today, after a few years of caring for her mother.

"I have so much to be grateful for!" Laurie says. "My Mom relies on me for everything, and the woman who once was very demanding and had to have things her way is now so appreciative and kind. She tells me she loves me and thanks me for the things I do for her. I never had that growing up, but God has allowed me to experience that now. It's because of the disease that my Mom has changed so much.

"My Mom continues to progress further away from us each day," Lau-rie says sadly. "From trying to figure out where the other sunglasses are (I spent 15 minutes trying to figure out why she was looking for another pair of sunglasses when she had one in her hand—you know, a 'pair'—she thought she needed two of them!) or helping her get her pants off that she's managed to not only put on inside-out but buttoned and zipped that way, you just never know what you're going to face next!"

By the grace of God, Laurie is able to look at her situation with a sense of humor. "It's always an adventure! Last week, my dad found her trying to watch Dr. Phil on the microwave in their kitchen. And there was the day when she cut the goose down blanket on her bed because she couldn't make it fit right; I'm still finding goose feathers around the house six months later! She will get lost in a store if you're not carefully watching; she makes terrible messes when she eats; she hates to bathe or shower; she says the most embarrassing things to people she meets; she falls easily…it's much like having a large toddler! It's just not nearly as fun; at least when you have a young one you know the child will eventually mature and learn to do things on his or her own. When you're caring for an aging parent who has Alzheimer's, you know the situation will only get worse. That parent is not going to go to school in a few years!"

Laurie admits there are days she wants to give up. "There have been times when I've been so weary and frustrated! I've gotten angry at having to clean up yet another mess (particularly the bathroom ones!). I've gotten frustrated trying to explain that it's not time to go out to dinner yet at three o'clock in the afternoon. I worry that she's going to fall and hurt herself or wander off and get lost. My heart breaks when I see her trying to use the TV remote as a telephone. I sometimes resent having to spend all day every Saturday, my day off, taking care of her so my Dad can have a break. Or having to use personal time off from work for her doctor's appointment because she insists something is terribly wrong because she has gas!

"And yet," Laurie continues, "God is *good*! He has taught me so much over the past five years, and He continues to grow and stretch me in ways I never imagined. I'm so thankful for the time I've had with my Mom these past few years. She is a happy person, and I'm grateful she is not suffering with physical pain. God has allowed me to maintain a sense of humor through it all; I have chosen to laugh rather than cry. My husband and children have been so supportive and loving to me and to my folks. I also believe I've become a better follower of Christ because I can now reach out to others who are struggling to care for their aging parents. The blessings are many! The rocky road is worth it! God is *good*!"

Can you say God is good in relation to the situation you desperately want changed? Maybe you can't say it right now. But as you begin to focus on the blessings that are in the midst of the bitterness, as Laurie has, God may change your perspective, too.

Laurie says, "I believe that in this day and time, many of us are facing or will soon face the challenge of aging parents. It's a tough struggle, and the rewards are few. But God is faithful, and He will carry us through even the most difficult days."

My Desperate Days

Hearing stories like Laurie's makes me think that my troubles are not nearly what I sometimes believe them to be.

For example, I remember a season in my life when I felt so frustrated, so desperate for a change. My teenage daughter, Dana, who is a lot like me in some ways, butts heads with me frequently. We both react emotionally, respond verbally, interrupt each other constantly, and get exasperated with each other. When my husband, Hugh, hears this going on, rather than intervening on my behalf, he scolds us both (or just me) as if we were two siblings. "Knock it off, you two" he will say to us. Or worse, he will just look at me and say, "Give it a rest."

One evening, I'd had it with that routine. I drove off crying because I wanted out of the frustration—away from my daughter, away from my husband, away from the house. *I just want to go somewhere far away*, I thought. *I am not appreciated. I am not feeling respected by my daughter. I am not feeling supported by my husband. I am not feeling understood or loved in the slightest.* (Now did you notice how many times I used the word *feeling* and how many times I used the pronoun *I*? We get that way when we're on the edge.)

Aware of how much my thoughts were focused on me, and yet still feeling I had grounds in the battle I was fighting, I desperately wanted to change—not just to have a change of circumstances, but *to change*. I desperately wanted wisdom for knowing how to respond to my daughter—and my husband—in a more mature way. I desperately wanted peace in my home. I desperately wanted to be able to redo some arguments we'd had. But mostly, I just wanted *out*.

I'm done with this! I shouted to God in my head. *I'm so done with this!*

What did that mean? I don't know. But it felt good to say it. Then I remembered my friend, Lara (from chapter 1), a friend who had gotten up and left because she was *done* with the frustrations at her home. Leaving was *not* what I really wanted to do. Why was I feeling so crazy? What was driving me so close to the edge?

Our Distress Call

I realize now why I was succumbing to the meltdown: 1) I was depending on my feelings, not the facts of the situation; 2) I was expecting *everyone else* around me to change, rather than looking at my own heart and actions; and 3) I was *listening* to the voices in my head rather than being the one who did the talking!

Today, I have a distress call—an SOS—that I turn to when I begin to feel like I'm going to go over the edge because certain things won't change. It's all about…

S—SORTING the facts from the feelings.

O—OFFERING my heart to the Lord for change.

S—STARTING to talk, rather than listen to, myself.

Sort the Facts from the Feelings

In my moment of frustration, I needed to ask myself, *What am I believing about God that isn't true?* I could best answer that question by comparing my thoughts and feelings to the facts:

- I was *feeling* that God had abandoned me as a mother and left me to figure this out on my own. But the fact is that God has promised that He will *never* leave me nor forsake me; therefore, He has not abandoned me as a mother (Hebrews 13:5).

- I was *feeling* hopeless in my situation. But the fact is that God promises He will work *all* things (even that difficult season with my daughter) for good to those who love Him and are called according to His purpose (Romans 8:28).

- I was *feeling* alone in my situation, as if God were unaware and unconcerned about my pain. But the fact is that God *is* aware of what I'm feeling at every moment. He has searched me and He knows me. He perceives my thoughts from afar. Before a word is on my tongue, He knows it completely (Psalm 139:1-4).

- I was *feeling* it was impossible for God to give me the kind of wisdom I needed to be a better mom, but the fact is that God *is* able to do so. James 1:5 says, "If any of you lacks wisdom, he should ask God, who gives generously to all without finding fault, and it will be given to him."

In other words, I had to look at the facts (about God's character) and not at what I was feeling.

Offer Your Heart to the Lord for Change

My prayer was not, "Change my daughter's heart." It was not, "Open my husband's eyes." Rather, I said, "God, grant me the discernment and the grace and the wisdom to respond to my daughter and husband in a way that draws a loving response out of them."

I realized I needed to look at myself and say, "God, show me what I need to do to be more like You," even though I was convinced that my daughter and husband were the problem that day. And even if they *were* the problem, my responsibility is to go to God and say, "In what way does *my* heart need to change so I can be more pleasing to You in this situation?"

The prayer, "Change *me,* God, not all of them" is usually the point at which real change starts. I am guilty, at times, of nagging God for change without asking Him to change me. Do you ever do that? Do your prayers sometimes sound like the following?

"God, change my husband" rather than "God, make me a more loving and desirable wife."

"God, change my child's attitude" rather than "God, help me to parent and respond in a way that draws loving responses out of my child."

"God, please provide us with more money" rather than "God, help us become better stewards of what You have already blessed us with."

"God, help me lose weight" rather than "God, give me the discipline to say no to certain foods and to work harder at buffeting my body and making it my slave."[12]

Start Talking to Yourself

Now you may be thinking, *If I start talking to myself, then I have* really *gone over the edge!* But I'd like you to start incorporating this principle in your life to *keep you* from going over the edge!

In his book *Desiring God,* John Piper suggests that we learn to preach to ourselves rather than listen. He quotes Dr. Martyn Lloyd-Jones as saying, "Have you realized that most of your unhappiness in life is due to the fact that you are listening to yourself instead of talking to yourself?"

He quotes Lloyd-Jones as saying that from the moment we rise in the morning, someone is talking to us. That voice in our heads is bringing back the problems of yesterday, planting fears in our hearts and minds about today, giving us insecurities about tomorrow. But we don't have to listen to those thoughts. They are often not even our own. We need to talk to those thoughts and straighten them out.[13]

We are told in 2 Corinthians 10:5 to "demolish arguments and every pretension that sets itself up against the knowledge of God" and to "take captive every thought to make it obedient to Christ." The reason we are to take every one of our thoughts captive is because they will wreak havoc in our lives if they are allowed to run loose. Bind them. Imprison them in the truth. Keep them from running rampant through your mind!

In Psalm 42, we see that the songwriter's solution to this problem was to start talking to himself:

> Why are you downcast, O my soul? Why so disturbed within me?
> Put your hope in God, for I will yet praise him, my Savior
> and my God (verse 5).

Instead of listening to his downcast soul, David started telling himself where to find hope. He told himself, "Put your hope in God, for I will yet praise him."

As you send out your SOS (**S**ort the facts from the feelings, **O**ffer your heart to the Lord for change, and **S**tart talking to yourself about what you should do), you will enable yourself to cling to the truth and not fall so easily over the edge.

Jesus on the Edge?

I use to wonder if Jesus was ever on-edge during the difficult situations in His life. After all, He had a group of 12 men with Him who just didn't seem to get it most of the time. They failed to see His true mission, they were often unbelieving, they all (not just Peter) denied knowing Him on the night He was arrested,[14] and all but one deserted Him as He died on the cross. All of that would have ticked me off. It would at least have made me edgy. Yet even in the worst that Jesus endured on earth—in His sufferings as well as in His everyday dealings with people—He was without sin. He didn't fall over the edge.

But He does know how you and I feel on the days we think we might go over the edge. Jesus—the Eternal Word—became flesh and dwelt among us and faced the frustrations we face. Thus, He can relate to us in all that we go through, too. I recently came across a prayer that thanks God for sending His Son in human form, and it reminds me of what the Savior had to cope with when He walked this earth:

> We thank you that Jesus did a day's work like any working-man, that he knew the problem of living together in a family, that he knew the frustration and irritation of serving the public, that he had to earn a living, and to face all the wearing routine of everyday work and life and living, and so clothed each common task with glory...

> We thank you that he knew what friendship means, that he had his own circle of [friends] whom he wanted to be with him, that he knew too what it means to be let down, to suffer from disloyalty and from the failure of love.

> We thank you that he too had to bear unfair criticism, prejudiced opposition, malicious and deliberate misunderstanding.

> We thank you that whatever happens to us, he has been there before, and that, because he himself has gone through things, he is able to help those who are going through them.

> Help us never to forget that he knows life, because he lived life, and that he is with us at all times to enable us to live victoriously.[15]

It's comforting to know that, according to Hebrews 4:15-16, we have a High Priest—Jesus, the One to whom we go to confess our sins—who understands all that we've been through and is able to help us get through everything we're still facing:

> We do not have a high priest who is unable to sympathize with our weaknesses, but we have one who has been tempted in every way, just as we are—yet was without sin. Let us then approach the throne of grace with confidence, so that we may receive mercy and find grace to help us in our time of need.

On those days that we're about to lose it, we need to remember that

Jesus knows and experienced the things in this life that can push us over the edge. He knew how to cope with it all, and far more than we'll ever deal with. So He certainly knows how to give us the strength we need so we can cope as well.

Lessons Learned in the Waiting Room

Let's visit our three on-the-edge women who dared to trust God with their circumstances and hold onto what they knew to be true of Him. Instead of flying the coop, they cried out to God for help and waited for His deliverance. But instead of changing their circumstances, God changed each of *them* and made them more able to deal with whatever now comes their way.

Kelly—who had vented in an e-mail about facing all sorts of obstacles, financial and otherwise—realizes that situations that roll in like a flood are a part of life. As desperate for change as Kelly was that morning, she is a woman who is grounded in the Word of God. She knows that when circumstances and the enemy do all they can to push her over the edge, she needs to make choices that would keep her in the spacious place of God's tender embrace. She wrote,

> At times, I'm desperate for change, but it doesn't come. I mean, we find ourselves wanting to get out of a situation, but we have to realize there will be another situation tomorrow. Life is about one thing after another. The situations that can send us over the edge may just keep coming. It's the world we live in.

Kelly realizes she has choices to make every day in the midst of life. And we do, too.

> If you keep focusing on yourself, you're gonna go down with it. You have a choice: Am I going to choose to focus on the circumstance, or am I going to choose to focus on the Lord and the fact that He has a place prepared for me?

Kelly often repeats to herself, "When things are happening and you don't know the answer, focus on what you *do* know. You *know* that God is good, that He has a plan, and that His ways are perfect."

Kelly keeps her focus on what she *does* know by staying grounded in the Word of God.

"I value my morning quiet time with the Lord," she said. "I *have* to have it. I do my devotions at a coffee shop. I take my Bible, a theology book, and a devotional. That time with God is what gets me through the day. It brings a peace and a calmness to my spirit so that even when things come up and they're crazy, that peace and calmness is still there."

Kelly has been involved in ministry, alongside her husband, for about 25 years. And that means she needs strength throughout the day to uphold not just herself, but others, too.

"I have to pray a lot. I'm really honest with the Lord—I talk to Him about what's going on. I don't pretend to feel a way that I don't feel. God knows anyway; who am I trying to fool?"

Pauline, who was frustrated at losing her teacher's aide, returned to her teaching job in the classroom, believing that she really *can* do all things through Christ, who strengthens her. And she's found herself stronger, more rested, and more able to trust the God who goes before her into all things:

> Things are so much better this year. I am learning to set limits
> and boundaries on my time. I am learning to make time for
> other things besides work. I am learning to trust God through
> the tough times and not wait until I am not coping.

Ingrid realized that to stick it out with God meant to stick it out with her husband, too. To exit her marriage on account of his struggle with pornography would be to say, "God is not big enough to fix this." She maintains hope in the One who goes before her into this once desperate but now workable situation:

> We have now gone to therapy and have gotten back together
> since. We're seeking help, individually and as a couple. I have
> found out that his heart was really not with the Lord and

that he was always showing faith to please me. I couldn't see a common yoke and I didn't know what reaction to take as a Christian woman. Things have improved now. We're working on maintaining our marriage. The Lord has given me forgiveness and I have decided that I cannot distrust my husband because it only poisons me, especially now that I changed jobs and I'm out of the house 12 hours a day! His sinful addiction is a battle he needs to fight on his own and I have totally put it in the Lord's hands, who is really working on him.

And the Lord is working on Ingrid, too. "For the first time in my life I feel total bliss, in every sense," she told me recently. "I'm well-balanced spiritually, emotionally, psychologically, financially, socially, and even physically! I have a deep peace that passes all understanding, and when I say this it brings tears of joy to my eyes.

"I know that life consists of ups and downs and that happiness is circumstantial, but the peace and joy don't go away. They are just dimmed sometimes. It's up to us, through our personal relationship with our Lord, to find them, dig them out, and enjoy them so we can experience life to its fullest.

"Jim has surrendered his addiction to the Lord. The total forgiveness I found for him, through the Lord, has humbled him. Through my sessions with my Christian counselors, I found out so many things about myself, faced them, solved them, and today feel so much older, but wiser and much happier. Not feeling responsible for Jim's addictions anymore has brought freedom to my mind, and I now thank God for having revealed this painful truth to me because it could have destroyed our marriage and us as individuals."

Getting Out of the Pit

When we are desperate for change, one of the choices before us is to stay in the place where we resent our circumstances. But doing that will only destroy us.

As one author so eloquently put it: "Self-pity is a slimy, bottomless pit. Once you fall in, you tend to go deeper and deeper into the mire. As you slide down those slippery walls, you are well on your way to depression, and the darkness is profound."[16]

Look at what happened to David, the psalmist, when he was in his slimy, bottomless pit of self-pity and sinking deeper into the mire. He *waited*. He waited patiently for the Lord. He stuck it out in his circumstances, and he received his deliverance:

> I waited patiently for the LORD;
>> he turned to me and heard my cry.
>
> He lifted me out of the slimy pit,
>> out of the mud and mire;
>
> He set my feet on a rock
>> And gave me a firm place to stand. [Sounds like he found his spacious place!]
>
> He put a new song in my mouth,
>> a hymn of praise to our God.
>
> Many will see and fear
>> and put their trust in the LORD (Psalm 40:1-3).

Did you notice the progression of events in that psalm? Desperation leads to deliverance when we become desperate for God. Then, once delivered, we become people of praise. Then others end up putting *their* trust in the Lord as a result of our song.

Your circumstances that you so want to change, dear friend, are building you into a living testimony of what God can do in and through your life. Your difficulties are driving you to a desperation for God that will cultivate in you a freedom and joy you never experienced before. No, you don't need to be desperate for change any longer. Be desperate, instead, for the One who never changes. He alone can set your feet on a rock and give you a firm place to stand.

Finding Your Spacious Place

You listened and pulled me from a lonely pit full
of mud and mire. You let me stand on a rock with
my feet firm, and you gave me a new song...

PSALM 40:1-3 CEV

Our desperation for things to change is a bottomless pit. As Kelly said, our present situations rarely change and new situations arise each day. To find our spacious place, we need to remember that God's mercies are new every morning (Lamentations 3:22-23). Develop a deeper trust in Him, and you'll be able to sing of His love forever...in spite of the things that may never change.

1. Think of a situation in your life that you are desperate to change. Now, practice sending out your distress call (your SOS) by completing the following. You may want to refer to the SOS points listed on pages 73–75 as a guide:

   Sort the Facts from the Feelings

   What are you feeling in your current situation?

   Now, what facts (about God's character or promises) apply to this situation?

   Offer Your Heart to the Lord for Change

   Write a prayer that reflects your desire for God to change *you* and your perspective, attitude, or response in this situation:

Start Talking to Yourself

What do you need to tell yourself in this situation so you can bring every thought captive to the obedience of Christ? (Feel free to use Scripture verses from this chapter or other ones you find helpful when you begin to slide down that slope of feeling hopeless.)

2. Psalm 42:6 says, "My soul is downcast within me; therefore I will remember You..." Depression creeps in when we forget God, and that life is all about revering Him and enjoying Him. Think of three ways you can "remember God" throughout the day and list them here:

   —

   —

   —

3. Read Psalm 40:1-3. Then fill in the blanks below so you have three praises you can begin singing *now* even though nothing in your situation has necessarily changed. (As you begin singing your praise, your life becomes a testimony to others of what God is doing in and through you.)

   • I will wait for You in my situation, God, because You are _____ and You are fully capable of _____
     _____.

   • Even though things might seem hopeless, I trust that You are _____
     _____.

   • You are God, and therefore You are _____,
     and I have no need to fear, worry, or stress.

5

Desperate for Love

DESIRING A FAITHFUL HEART

If I find in myself a desire which no experience in
this world can satisfy, the most probable explanation
is that I was made for another world.

C.S. LEWIS

Satisfy us in the morning with your unfailing love,
that we may sing for joy and be glad all our days.

PSALM 90:14

Michelle was 13 years old when her parents separated and her mother moved away from home. Two years later, her mother died and her father didn't know what to do with the children. That was when she first noticed that she was desperate for love.

"For many years I tried to fill the emptiness with men," Michelle said. "At the beginning of each relationship, I knew they weren't good for me. But I would've rather been with someone who treated me badly than be alone." She ended up marrying young so she could get out of the house.

"I wanted so badly to be loved that I married at 17. He was 19. I wanted someone to love me, I wanted a place to live, and I wanted to have kids. We had two children, but even that couldn't keep us together."

That marriage and a subsequent one both ended in disaster. With six children by then, Michelle married a third husband. Together they found God when disaster hit—in the form of a back injury as she was eight months pregnant with her seventh child. She and her family ended up losing nearly everything they had. Then a local Salvation Army branch

ministered to them, providing Christmas gifts to their children and showing them the love and grace of God.

Today, at 46, Michelle is no longer desperate for a man, or for love, or
for a sense of purpose. "Today I am desperate for God," she says. "More
of Him, more of His presence, more of His Word." Michelle's life proves
that when you get to a place where you have *nothing*, you can more read-
ily see God as your *everything*.

Hillary has longed for love all of her life, too. But this 30-year-old
married woman has not looked for a husband to fill the void in her life.
It was the love of her parents that she felt she never had.

"I have always longed for both the acceptance and approval from my
family of origin," Hillary says. "I was the black sheep in my family; no
matter what I did, how religious I was, or how I performed, I never felt
unconditional love or that I was good enough. There was a lot of abuse
in my family.

"As the oldest of eleven children, I found it very difficult to understand
how parents, and then God, could love each of us individually for who
we were and not lose us in the shuffle. I desperately longed for that feeling of true love—not a love based on the fact that I performed in a certain way—through behavior or religion, and so on. What if I had done
something really bad? Would they have still loved me then?"

Years of depression and feeling suicidal drove Hillary to begin a quest
for God's healing. But when she understood that God loved her, the issues
from her past affected her understanding of God's love. "This [baggage
from her past] translated into my walk with God—I felt as though I was
required to behave or perform in order for Him to love me. It has taken
my entire life to realize that God loves me not for my doing, but for my
being. I still struggle to wrap my head around that truth."

Sonya's quest for marriage led her down a road of dismay. She believed
God had given her visions of the man she would marry: a man of God
who was in full-time ministry, someone who would love her and her

children as his own, someone who would provide for her and protect her in every way.

"Well, I found such a man," she says. "But I failed to realize he would be just that—a man—and man is not perfect and possesses many faults. In the end I was emotionally spent, financially drained, and spiritually bankrupt."

That Deep Well Within Us

There is perhaps no more driving desperation than that of a woman to be loved. Our longing for love lies at the root of nearly every desperation we have, doesn't it? And yet this longing of ours—to be loved unconditionally and sacrificially for who we are—has already been met by the One who has loved us beyond measure. If we could just grasp it, see it in the gestures God makes toward us every day, it would change how we live.

Let me tell you about another woman who longed for love until she found Jesus standing right in front of her.

This woman had one man after another in her life. She had married so many times that she probably thought, *Why get married at all?* and evidently had decided to just live with—and not marry—her most recent boyfriend. Maybe that way he wouldn't feel obligated to her and he would stay around longer. But having him in her life still wasn't enough for her. And she found herself alone, and still thirsting for more.

We find this woman in the Bible. She is known only as "the Samaritan woman." But she sounds like a lot of women today, doesn't she?

When she saw Jesus at the well, Jesus surprised her by breaking both cultural and gender barriers and asking her to draw some water for Him. Her response was cynical: "'You are a Jew and I am a Samaritan woman. How can you ask me for a drink?' (For Jews do not associate with Samaritans)" (John 4:9).

Jesus responded by hinting to her that He was the One she was really thirsting for in her quest to be satisfied. "If you knew the gift of God and who it is that asks you for a drink, you would have asked him and he would have given you living water," He said.

Her reply tells more about her than she might have realized: "Sir... you have nothing to draw with and *the well is deep.* Where can you get this living water?"

While the woman was speaking about an actual water well, there was another deep well...within her. A deep well of longings that had not been satisfied. And her skepticism showed that perhaps she was unwilling to fall for another man with another empty promise.

I believe Jesus' response to her is a response to every one of our longing hearts today:

> Everyone who drinks this water will be thirsty again, but whoever drinks the water I give him will never thirst. Indeed the water I give him will become in him a spring of water welling up to eternal life (John 4:13-14).

Jesus was telling her that everyone who seeks satisfaction from a physical—and temporary—well in this world will remain unsatisfied. They'll constantly come up dry. In other words, every woman who went where the Samaritan woman had gone to find her fulfillment would remain unsatisfied. But when they drink of the water *H*e has to offer, they will experience true fulfillment and receive eternal life.

We don't know if the Samaritan woman took Jesus up on His offer to quench her deep-down thirst. But we do know that when the woman and Jesus were interrupted by the return of Jesus' 12 disciples, she quickly left to tell everyone in her neighborhood, "Come, see a man who told me everything I ever did. Could this be the Christ?" (verse 29). And when she departed, she left her empty water jar at the well. I'd like to think that empty jar represented her empty heart and she left it there because she'd finally found the only One who can satisfy.[17]

Alexandria's Search for Love

While teaching at a retreat a couple years ago, a striking woman in her late forties came up to me after one of my sessions and took hold of my hand and said seven words that piqued my interest: "I was the woman at the well."

I told her I wanted to hear her story.

"All my life I have longed for love," Alexandria told me. "My first real love was Jesus, but I did not believe He could provide for my financial and emotional needs." Interestingly, she trusted God for her *eternal* life, but not with her *everyday* life. Because of that she desperately sought a husband, and each time she married, she settled for less.

At 18, Alexandria married her boyfriend because she had become sexually involved with him. "I was ashamed of it and wanted to make it right, so we married." Her marriage lasted 12 years despite her being physically and emotionally abused. After some extramarital affairs on his part, her husband left the marriage.

After he departed, Alexandria was afraid of being alone. "I went with the first man I met after my husband left. I was angry with God and told Him He had let me down. I believed my motives were right and yet I wasn't loved. I told God, 'I trusted You and You let me down. Now I'm going to live life my way.'

"Don't ever, *ever* say that to God," Alexandria warns, in hindsight. Her decision to live life her way only led to deeper despair.

Alexandria's next relationship was with a man much older than her. He was kind and tried to break off the relationship, but she was still afraid to be alone. "Out of that relationship, I got pregnant with baby number four. At that time I had recommitted my life to Christ and was convicted that the relationship wasn't right. I went before my church, confessed the baby conceived out of wedlock, and then summoned the strength to break off the relationship."

But once Alexandria had the baby and got her figure back, men approached her again and she began dating. Although by this time she was more discreet and didn't bring men home or live with any, she still compromised her convictions. One day her heart was broken by a man with whom she had a relationship because he admitted to her he was legally married, but separated from his wife. "I was mortified," she said. "I fell to my knees and said 'God, Your Word really *is* right. I've tried to rewrite the rules, but I've learned now that Your way is right.'"

After Alexandria prayed that prayer, she read a book on sanctification and realized she needed to keep her body pure for her Lord. "That was my turning point of true repentance," she said. "I changed my phone number. And my life started going better."

Alexandria got a job working for a Christian television station and met a man whom another woman said would make a good husband. "Some red flags of warning rose up in my mind, but I didn't want to let this woman down by not being in a relationship with this man." Because it was a long-distance relationship, Alexandria didn't have the opportunity to get to know the man well before she married him. Shortly after they married, she started noticing patterns of him not being around very much. "We were married for four years, and then he had an affair." He had also been violent toward Alexandria and her children. She left him.

After her second divorce, she began praying for a husband again. She had just bought a home and began to see a need for a father for her 13-year-old son. She now regrets that she didn't see God as the perfect father to her son.

Alexandria then met a widower who was financially stable. She promised God she wouldn't have sex outside of marriage anymore. Yet she failed in that promise and married this man after knowing him only a month.

"I got to the place where I felt we should get married or break up. I proposed breaking up, and he said, 'Let's get married.' I remember thinking, *This could be the last boat going to China. I was 44 years old, and here was a man who wanted to marry me.*"

They married, and at first everything seemed okay. But about two years later, she got a call at work and discovered her husband had been accused of sexual inappropriateness with a minor.

"Initially I forgave him, tried to work with him, got him some accountability, and we set boundaries. But nothing changed," she said. They were divorced shortly after.

"At that point I said, 'Enough! I need to look to God now.'"

Alexandria describes the commitment she made to the Lord and how it changed her life: "I came to the decision that I need to stay single. I had to ask God to change my heart. I was in a type of relationship addiction. I asked God to take that out of me. I needed to see men as fallen people with faults"—and not as gods who could solve her problems and fill her up.

Alexandria had long been desperate for a man more times than she could count. But today she is desperate for God.

"I want the Lord to be who and what I need, emotionally. I know I'm a healthy person now, but I'm aware of my weaknesses. So I've made a decision to seek the Lord every day, consistently, and to stay in the Word. When Jesus said, 'When you drink of the water I give you, you'll never thirst again,' I have to believe, on a daily basis, that the more of myself I give to the Lord and truly believe He is the living water, then the more I will be able to see a man as any other person—not as a god in my life."

Because Alexandria knows where her weaknesses lie, she has chosen to not read romance novels or watch romantic movies that might stir certain desires or the temptation to want something more than what she has in her relationship with God. She has also placed boundaries around her life: "I have to keep myself full of good activities. I'm studying for a doctorate in ministry, taking music lessons to learn how to play the piano, and working with a choir. When I'm accountable to other people, I do okay."

Alexandria says she must continually stay in the Word to keep her focus on Christ and to keep from sinking into guilt or shame from her past. "In all my mistakes and idolatry related to men, Christ has shown me that He loves me and forgives me." Alexandria says she now lives by Romans 8:1: "There is now no condemnation for those who are in Christ Jesus."

"I used to think I was a victim in terms of what had been done to me in my relationships. I believed I was honest, had the right motives, and so on. But now I see that I, too, was responsible for the failed relationships because I made the wrong choices when it came to men."

Now, when it comes to love, Alexandria says, "Jesus is the greatest choice I've ever made. Three times I married men whom the Lord had said no to. The first one was physically abusive, the second a womanizer and addict, and the third, a predator. When my third marriage ended in divorce, I knew my thinking needed to change so as not to repeat the same pattern again. I want Jesus Christ to be my all in all—to be enough for me."

Today, at 50, Alexandria is no longer on the edge seeking to be loved. She is, instead, on the edge for the One who loves her beyond reason.

"Now I am seeing Jesus as more than enough. I am boldly sharing the truth of God's Word. I feel so deeply loved by God and am able to share that love with the women I serve on a daily basis." As a life-skills training manager for a Christian organization, Alexandria has opportunities every day to let women know they are loved by the One who loves her as well.

A Different Kind of Love

Alexandria's history showed she was desperate for a man—much like the Samaritan woman. Sometimes this meant settling for *any* man...as long as there was *someone* in her life. I know many women who feel it is better to be with someone who makes them miserable than to be alone. I have even heard women say, "It's better to share him with another woman, than to not have him at all!" Oh the desperation we have for what we believe is "love."

As women, we have been known to resort to foolish, even crazy, behavior out of a desperation for love: becoming pregnant to try to "save" a relationship, tattooing our bodies with a boyfriend's name to show him how "committed" we are, enduring secret physical or emotional pain so we can hold onto someone, having one meltdown after another because our needs aren't being met or we don't *feel* loved. We even search out father figures in men and boyfriends, looking for the love we never felt from our own father. But why are we never that desperate for *God's* love?

God loves you more "desperately" than anyone ever could. And He did some pretty radical things to show it:

- "See, I have engraved you on the palms of my hands," God says in Isaiah 49:16. God has *tattooed* us on His palms! That is desperate.

- "I am now going to allure her; I will lead her into the desert and speak tenderly to her" (Hosea 2:14). He strategizes to get us back. That is desperate.

- He counts the number of hairs on our heads (Matthew 10:30), records our days in a book (Psalm 139:16), and saves our tears in a bottle (Psalm 56:8 NASB). Now *that* is desperate...almost obsessive!

If we took a good long look at what love really is, we would recognize that it's right in front of us—and we wouldn't be so easily seduced by the substitutes.

God's Love Is Eternal

Unlike anyone on this earth, God has *always* known you. And He has always loved you. In the Bible, God tells us, through the prophet Jeremiah, "I have loved you with an everlasting love; I have drawn you with loving-kindness" (Jeremiah 31:3).

An everlasting love. That means there was no beginning to it and there's no end to it, either. It always was. It always will be. That is endless love.

God's love is unlike anything we can experience from people on this earth. My husband loves me, and has promised to for the rest of my life, but he has not *always* loved me. For the first 26 years of his life, he didn't even know me. My parents have loved me since the day I was born. But one day they will depart from this earth. They cannot love me from the grave. Love that will endure forever can only come from the One who has no beginning and no end.

God's Love Is Enduring

Over the past several months, several women I know have had their husbands walk out on them. They were left explaining to others what happened to their "love":

> "He decided, after thirty years of marriage, that he just doesn't want to be married anymore."

> "He told me he never really loved me, but was just going through the motions."

> "My husband told me he's had secrets that he can no longer live with, so he wants to make a fresh start without me."

Tragically, it happens. We get burned by a selfish example of what someone thinks is "love" or "a loss of love." But just because one who professed to love you fails miserably doesn't mean that God's love is any less sincere. God's everlasting love waits to pick you up, bind your wounds, and place you on the path of life again...a redeemed, restored life in which you will experience what true love really is:

> "Your Maker is your husband—the LORD Almighty is his name—the Holy One of Israel is your Redeemer; he is called the God of all the earth. The LORD will call you back as if you were a wife deserted and distressed in spirit—a wife who married young, only to be rejected," says your God. "For a brief moment I abandoned you, but with deep compassion I will bring you back. In a surge of anger I hid my face from you for a moment, but with everlasting kindness I will have

compassion on you," says the LORD your Redeemer (Isaiah 54:5-8).

God spoke those words through the prophet Isaiah, to His people, Israel, who had continually turned their backs on Him. Yet God kept coming back for them, as a lovesick husband seeking the return of his wife. In many ways, you and I are like the unfaithful nation of Israel when it comes to seeking love and fulfillment outside of the realm of God's love. We search for love, we think we must have a man to complete us, and yet God stands waiting to be our Faithful Husband if we would just look to Him first to meet our needs.

God's words to His people, Israel, apply to those of us today who have trusted in His Son, Jesus, for our salvation. And so we, too, can bank on His promise to bring back—with deep compassion—those who have been "deserted and distressed in spirit."

God's love is eternal *and* enduring. Can any love on this earth compare? Not a chance. Only the God of the universe can love you in that passionate, pursuing way.

Could the realization that the living God of this universe loves you passionately make you want to grab hold of that love and live differently? Could it make you desperate not for the love of someone else, but to love Him in return?

My friend, if we became desperate for God with the same kind of passion with which He is desperate for us, we would experience the kind of love that liberates, not suffocates. So don't you think it's time to be free?

Developing a Faithful Heart

Let's look at some of the ways we can develop a faithful heart for God. As we begin to love Him, over anyone else, He will develop in us a desperation for *His* love...and we will know what it means to be on the edge for *Him* and not for anyone else—ever.

Love Him by Letting Go of the Idols

Jesus said we are to love God with all our heart, soul, mind, and strength (Mark 12:30). But what does that look like? I believe that means we're to be totally consumed with love for God. It means He is all we think about, He is the One we sing about, He is the One we seek to please, He is the One we live for. It's a lot like being *in love.* Yet the idols in our life often get this type of devotion from us instead.

In her book *Idols of the Heart* author Elyse Fitzpatrick says,

> Idols aren't just stone statues. No, idols are the thoughts, desires, longings, and expectations that we worship in the place of the true God. Idols cause us to ignore the true God in search of what we think we need. If we think we need to be loved, more than we need a thriving relationship with God, then we have made the idea of love an idol that we worship over God. We can make other people our gods, too, by loving them more than Him.

Having godly relationships is a blessing and a source of happiness, and there is nothing sinful in desiring them. But if they are the source of our joy, if they take top priority in our lives, then they are our gods, Fitzpatrick says.[18]

Idols creep into our lives and wrap themselves around our hearts without us even realizing it. Sonya (who was left emotionally spent, financially drained, and spiritually bankrupt after marrying who she thought was "the perfect godly man") is an example of this. She said that after much prayer and crying out to God, she rededicated her life completely to Christ.

"God began to show me there were parts of my life I was withholding from Him, and these had become idols," Sonya said. "When I lined up the simple things in my life such as conversations, what I was reading, and my friends to the Word of God, I found my relationship with Christ wasn't what I thought it was. My prayer became, 'Lord, show me how to put You first and change me from the inside out.' Although I was comfortable with being single, there was still this small piece of me that felt I needed to be married. It wasn't until I began to change my mindset and truly seek God that I was able to combat those idols."

Love Him by Loving Others

Jesus said, "If you love me, you will obey what I command" (John 14:15). Six verses later He said, "Whoever has my commands and obeys them, he is the one who loves me" (verse 21). Then in verse 23 He said,

"If anyone loves me, he will obey my teaching." And He said that yet again in John 15:10: "If you obey my commands, you will remain in my love." Shortly thereafter He said, "You are my friends if you do what I command" (verse 14). Then He summed it all up: "*This* is my command: Love each other" (verse 17). Jesus was serious about us showing our love to Him by loving others unconditionally and in a way that seeks their best, not our own. In 1 John 5:3, the apostle John, who recorded Jesus' commands to us, restated this mandate once again: "This is love for God: to obey his commands. And his commands are not burdensome."

Finally, our love relationship with God is put to the test by how we love others:

> Dear friends, let us love one another, for love comes from God. Everyone who loves has been born of God and knows God. Whoever does not love does not know God, because God is love...since God so loved us, we also ought to love one another. No one has ever seen God; but if we love one another, God lives in us and his love is made complete in us (1 John 4:7-8,11-12).

What would a woman's life look like if she were to direct her desperation to be loved into a desperation to love others? She would not exhibit a selfish love that seeks what it can get in return, but an unconditional, godly love that says to others, "I give up my life for yours, as an imitation of what Christ did when He laid down His life for me."

Love Him by Living Right

When we are truly in love, we easily submit to the wishes of the one whom we love, especially if we trust his love and protection of us. By submitting to the Holy Spirit's control over our lives, we are saying, "I love You, God, and I trust You immensely." In Ephesians 4:1 the apostle Paul urged us to "live a life worthy of the calling you have received," and we can best do that when we yield ourselves to the Holy Spirit and take on the "fruit" or character of God's Spirit, which includes love, joy, peace, patience, kindness, goodness, faithfulness, gentleness, and self-control (Galatians 5:22-23). That list should be written out before us and posted on our refrigerator, desk, car, or wherever we will see it often. It reminds us of the characteristics of Jesus—and the characteristics we, too, can possess and display when we yield control of our lives to Him.

Love Him by Lifting Him Up

Admit it: When you love someone, you can't stop talking about that person. You praise his good qualities and you become overly focused on what he does *right*. God deserves your praise, adoration and thanksgiving far more than any human on this earth. So bring it on! In fact, on days when I am feeling complacent, out of sorts, angry with myself or someone else, or just plain indifferent, I've found that as I begin to praise God, my focus shifts wholly from me to Him, from pity to praise, from my measly existence to His majestic presence.

Try it right now and see what it does for your heart:

> Because your love is better than life,
>   my lips will glorify you.
> I will praise you as long as I live,
>   and in your name I will lift up my hands
>   (Psalm 63:3-4).

Choosing Which Way We'll Go

Bonnie realized that when her husband of 38 years left her, she could be driven toward a desperation to find another man, or driven toward a desperation for the God who can redeem and restore all things. She is choosing to cling to the Maker and Sustainer of her soul so she won't fall off the edge.

"It is incredibly hard for me to be single," she says. "I loved being married and miss the companionship, even though my marriage was far from what I wanted it to be. But I have made an absolute vow to God not to fill this void with anything ungodly.

"I am reeling from the rejection and betrayal and abandonment that I have experienced. But I do not want to relieve the pain by making bad choices.

"My pain has absolutely driven me to 'soak up' the Lord. I am clinging to the Word now. The greatest source of strength and comfort for me is knowing that God's Word is true. I can have absolute confidence in God's promises and claim them for myself. When God says, 'Do not fear' all the way through His Word, I know that I have no reason to fear. I have also become a frequent listener to online sermons in the middle of the night when I can't sleep."

Bonnie is letting God redeem this pain in her life so she can be used by Him in a greater way: "Even in my desperation, my 'freedom' and walking in faith has opened the door for me to minister to co-workers and other single women," she says.

Bonnie has "four beautiful, godly sons and many wonderful Christian sisters who are a great support to me. My desperation for God has resulted in His showing His great faithfulness to me."

But can you show such faithfulness to God even when it appears He is saying no to what you want in the realm of love?

When God Says No

Because God loves us and wants to prosper us (Jeremiah 29:11), we tend to think that means when we want a man, God will bring one to us. And we think that as long as the man loves God, we will automatically receive God's blessing. But that's not necessarily the case. God is not obligated to bring a man into our lives simply because we think that will make us happy. My friend, Dawn Marie, learned this, and is so glad she did.

Dawn Marie, who is now in her late fifties, was longing to find a godly husband when she was in her early twenties. While working for a revival ministry, she met a Christian man whom she believed was God's best for her. She began pouring her life into the relationship and ignored some of the warning signs that this man was not the best for her after all. When she challenged this man about some spiritual issues, he broke off the relationship.

"I was heartbroken," said Dawn Marie. "But a mentor challenged me to turn the negative situation into something positive." Her mentor told her, "You're feeling desperate right now, but God has a purpose in this." He turned Dawn Marie's heartbreaking situation into a project for her. He asked her to write a list of what she wanted in a husband and start focusing on being the kind of woman who would attract that kind of man. Daily she began to pray for what she wanted in a husband and what she wanted to become so she could be the wife God wanted her to be. She began focusing not on *finding* the right one, but on *being* the right one. During that time she grew in her love relationship with God. Exactly one year to the date of writing her list, she met the man who is now her husband, who fit the bill!

"The men I was dating before were what I thought I wanted. But God gave me what I needed," she said.

It doesn't always happen that way, but perhaps God wanted to make sure He was first in Dawn Marie's heart before He let another man come around. And He apparently honored her choice to wait on Him for *His* best for her, not her idea of what she thought was best.

"I was so desperate for love in my twenties that I almost ended up in a loveless marriage," she said. "God rescued me before I made that foolish choice, even though it broke my heart at the time. I almost missed God's best for me in love because I was so determined in my own manipulation of circumstances.

"I learned a valuable lesson: It is more important to love, fear, and obey God than get all my 'desires' fulfilled—and yet, when I do love, fear, and obey Him, He satisfies my desires first with Himself, and then He either changes my desires or gives blessings that I couldn't even imagine to seek for myself. He knows what is best."

Let Him Find You

So the choice is yours. Would you rather chase after love that may one day let you down? Or will you be content in the arms of the One who lavishes love on you and shows Himself to be faithful in every way? Start investing in the search that yields true treasure.

God's Word tells us that when we search for Him, we'll find Him— often because He is the One who finds us: "You will seek me and find me when you seek me with all your heart (Jeremiah 29:13).

O my friend who longs for love…long for *Him!* Search for Him as one searches for treasure, and let Him find you, bind you up, and redeem you into a woman fully satisfied with a heart that beats for Him alone.

Finding Your Spacious Place

I trust your love, and I feel like celebrating
because you rescued me.
PSALM 13:5 CEV

If we are desperate for *anyone* else's love over God's, we are on a dangerous road toward devastation. But if we strive to love Him above all, we will find freedom—that spacious place in His embrace—rather than feel on the edge when it comes to love.

1. Read Psalm 18:1-2, which includes descriptions of God and His love for you. Write a prayerful response to God after each of the following descriptions:

   He is your rock:

   He is your fortress:

   He is your deliverer:

   He is your shield:

   He is your stronghold:

2. Read 1 Corinthians 13:4-7. This passage describes God's love toward you, as well as the kind of love He wants you to show toward others. Which of these characteristics, specifically, do you need to focus on showing toward others as a way of showing your love for God?

3. On a scale of 1-10 (1 being completely indifferent and 10 being completely consumed), how would you rate your passion for God? (Circle one.)

1   2   3   4   5   6   7   8   9   10

Spend some time in prayer, asking God to develop in you a heart that desires Him alone. Confess the times your heart has chased after other loves (people, possessions, interests, money, career goals, etc.) and ask Him to cultivate in you a heart of faithfulness toward Him—the same kind of faithfulness He has displayed toward you.

6

Desperate to Avoid the Patterns of the Past

DESIRING A NEW LEGACY

Therefore, if anyone is in Christ, [she] is a new
creation; the old has gone, the new has come!

2 CORINTHIANS 5:17

've been told there is within each of us a time bomb that is ticking.
Traumatic events from childhood that we've buried in the back of our
minds tick away at our present sanity. Pain from past relationships
that we've shoved down deep and refused to deal with ticks away unbe-
knownst to us. Things we should've said but never did tick away...tick
tick, tick tick...until we reach a certain age—or a certain place in life—
and then we blow!

"We all have issues in our past that we need to deal with," a woman
told me one afternoon after I asked how she was doing. She was seeing a
therapist who was helping her to work through some issues from childhood. Yet she didn't appear to be any healthier or happier than when she
started the process of delving into her past pain.

I've been told by another friend that there are situations in everyone's
past—including my own—that need to be dealt with before we can become
completely whole. I've had relatives tell me there are probably things in
my past that I don't even remember that I should come to terms with.
And I've heard "counselors" (and what my husband calls "religious feel-
good psychiatrists") on television say that when we look inside at who we
really are—the good, the bad, and the ugly—and learn to love ourselves,
we can begin the process toward healing and wholeness.

Feeling confused and a little depressed, I sat down for breakfast with Chris, a close friend who is the most stable, wise, and spiritually mature woman I know. *She is certainly never on the edge,* I thought.

As we sat talking, I asked Chris how she held it all together. Did *she* have a time bomb ticking away in *her,* too? Has she dug into the past so she could face her future? It was upon asking those questions that I finally learned her story. And I realized that if anyone had past issues to deal with, it would be her.

Chris was the oldest of six children and was raised by parents who didn't look to God for the answer to life's troubles. Therefore, her upbringing was anything but stable. In fact, it was shaky and unpredictable. At times, it was even scary.

"I saw my mom on the edge several times," she told me. "She was carted away in a straitjacket once. She had three nervous breakdowns that I know of."

Chris was 20 years old at the time her mother was admitted to a psychiatric hospital. Chris didn't know God personally at that time and she remembers the despairing feeling: *This is my legacy. This is how I'm going to turn out someday.*

Chris visited her mother in the psychiatric ward and was horrified to discover that she actually seemed happy there. She was free from her responsibilities as a parent; she had no pressures on her. She was being taken care of. And she was at peace.

Angry at what she saw happening and at what appeared to be her own destiny, Chris reprimanded her mother: "I told her, 'You're not staying here. I'm not going to raise your kids.'"

Chris' mother eventually left the psych ward and came home. But within a year she was diagnosed with cancer, and she went on to endure three grueling years of treatment. During that time Chris lived at home, caring for her mother and her siblings. By the time Chris was 23 her mother passed away, and Chris tried to step into the role of caregiver at her home. But tensions arose quickly between Chris and her father, so she moved out shortly afterward.

Looking back now on her mother's emotionally up-and-down life, Chris realizes her mother had known many unmet expectations. She was a woman on the edge, a woman who was frustrated that she didn't get to do what she wanted to do with her life. She had also had disappointments in her marriage. She was, in some ways, like you and me.

Today, Chris is the same age her mom was when she died of cancer. "I've been without her longer than I've been with her," Chris says. And she lives with the knowledge that she has the choice to repeat the mistakes of the past, or create a new legacy.

Chris has chosen to chart a new course. As a wife and mother of two grown stepchildren and one preteen son, she is sure of one thing: By the grace of God she will not repeat the dysfunctional patterns of her past.

"Because I have that in my makeup, I've made a pact with myself: I will never let myself get that crazy. I never want my children to see the drama I saw when I was growing up. It's traumatic. Sure, there are times in my life when I feel I'm going to lose it. But I tell myself, 'You don't want to go there.'"

What Keeps Us Sane?

So what keeps Chris—a woman with a "genetic tendency" to lose it— from going over the edge? What makes this woman more sane, mentally and emotionally, than most of us who *don't* have mental illness haunting our past? Chris cited some practices in her life that can serve as "sanity steps" in our lives, too, when we feel we're going to lose it.

Fill Up on the Word of God Daily

Four years after her mother passed away, Chris married Dan. And six years into their marriage, Chris and Dan received Christ as their personal Savior through the influence of Dan's two preteen children who had come to live with them. Chris learned early on in her Christian life to look to the Word of God, not the wisdom of the world, as her guide and counselor. Because advice from the world would rush in every day, she needed a mind fully saturated in the Word of God in order to discern the voice of truth. Chris says when she hears that voice in her head—the voice of the enemy or maybe just her own fearful, unbelieving thoughts— she has to counter that voice with truth from God's Word.

"When you feel like you're going to lose it, listen to the truth," Chris says. "No, you're not gonna lose it. You have been given a sound mind. It's never as bad as it feels at the moment."

Reciting Scripture (or rereading it if you don't yet have it memorized) will get it ingrained into your head so it is louder than the selfish or worldly thoughts that bombard you every day.

And once Scripture has penetrated her heart and mind, Chris will regain her perspective. She will walk through her house and see photos of her three children—all of whom love the Lord—and will remember she has a husband who is dependable and faithful, and she will ask herself, "Now *why* were you going to lose it? What is so bad?"

We can fill up on the Word of God by studying Scripture, listening to sermons from the Word of God, reading the Word out loud (so we hear it as well as read it), listening to worship music that includes Scripture, and so on. But just reading and studying Scripture isn't enough. We also need role models in front of us.

Find a Trusted Woman Who Can Mentor You

Chris' mother did not serve as a spiritual role model for Chris. Later, when Chris surrendered her life to the Lord at the age of 35, she didn't have an older Christian woman in her life to mentor her. So she searched the Scriptures and found a role model there. She sought to imitate a woman in Scripture whom most of us feel intimidated by. She looks to the "wife of noble character" who is described in Proverbs 31:10-31.

"Some people make fun of the Proverbs 31 woman," Chris says. "Some women feel intimidated by her. But I really do aspire to be like her."

By placing her life up against the description of the excellent wife in Proverbs 31, Chris has had a standard to which she can compare herself and a goal to which she can aspire. In Proverbs 31, we find a woman who...

- faithfully cares for her husband

- works hard to maintain the well-being of her home and family

- invests and manages money well

- extends help to the poor and needy

- speaks wisely and instructs others faithfully

- garners the praise of her husband and children

- keeps a positive outlook on life

Upon seeing how the Proverbs 31 woman served others, Chris realized that just because she didn't have a mentor herself didn't mean she couldn't mentor others. And by being a mentor to other women and seeing how they benefitted from the relationship of trust, transparency, and accountability, she encouraged women to seek out a mature woman in the faith whom they could trust.

"I think a lot of women feel isolated," Chris says. "And the enemy enjoys playing on that. When we feel isolated and don't talk about what we're struggling with and how we're feeling, it becomes dangerous."

Like me, Chris learned that even if you don't have a mentor available to you, it's good to become one. I remember a time in my own life when I was frustrated that I didn't have a spiritual mentor. My husband had just become the senior pastor of a small country church in which I was the youngest woman physically and the oldest woman spiritually. I remember crying out to God many times to bring someone alongside me who could be a spiritual encouragement to me. But God impressed upon my heart the need to *be* that person in someone *else's* life. As I started a Bible study and began to teach the Word to the women in my church, God brought—not from my church, but from an organization called the Network of Evangelical Women in Ministry (NEWIM)—*several* seasoned women of God into my life to encourage, support, and mentor me. I have never doubted God's ability to give us what we need when we need it and supply us with what we need to *be* the mentor to another woman if that's what is required of us first.

Focus on Serving Others, Not Yourself

Chris found that when she was living for herself she was more likely to go off the edge. But when she was serving others, she was no longer self-focused.

"God wants much of me. He wants my mind, my self-control. There's not enough time in life to be focused on just me. I find when I'm serving others there's not much time left to be focused on myself."

Being others-focused is another trait Chris saw in the Proverbs 31 woman, who made a priority of her husband and children and helped others in need.

Focusing on others also gives us a sense of accountability. Chris is the leader of a group of praying moms, a leader in the college women's group at her church, a woman people look to for advice, a woman who has discipled and continues to disciple many single women and young moms. With so many people looking to her for strength, she is constantly reminded of the people she would let down if she gave in to her feelings and flew off the edge.

"I have a strong sense that God wants more from me than that," she says. "There's a certain level of expectations that others have of me. I'd be failing a lot of people who look up to me."

Fix Your Gaze Forward

Chris is challenged by the Proverbs 31 woman to be one who "can laugh at the days to come" (verse 25). When we are focused on the past we tend to look at regrets, pain, and things we can't change. But to look forward is to anticipate what God will do in our lives. The excellent wife in Proverbs 31 "can laugh at the days to come" not merely because she's prepared for them, but because she realizes she has a bright and hopeful future. She knows the One who goes before her into the future. Chris often asks herself, "Am I really looking forward to all that God has for me?" She wants to be forward-focused and not delve backward at what used to be. She wants to look expectantly to what God has for her in the future.

God's Word instructs us in Philippians 3:13-14 to forget "what is behind" and strain "toward what is ahead" and press on "toward the goal to win the prize" of the upward call of God in Christ Jesus. As we forget our past pains and look forward to where God is leading us, we *can* press on toward the prize of His call on us—the prize of becoming more like Him.

Rely on God's Power to Change

To fill up on God's Word, find a mentor to whom you can be account-able, focus on serving others, and fix our gaze forward does not come naturally to us. All that requires us to rely on God's power, rather than our own, to accomplish the work we cannot do ourselves.

Chris recalls several times in her life—both before she knew God and even during her growing years with God—that she was not others-focused. She lived to please herself. And she enjoyed it at times. But she now relies on God's strength to do through her what she can't do on her own. She cites Philippians 4:13 as a key verse for her life: "I really believe I *can* do all things—including not going over the edge—through Christ, who strengthens me," she says. "I really *can* have my husband's ex-wife,

Eleanor—whom I saw as my enemy for many years—in my kitchen enjoying a cup of coffee with me and relating with me as a sweet sister in Christ."

"You really *can* love your children when they're not living as you want them to."

"You really *can* love your husband even in the times he is not attractive to you."

"You really *can* love others who say things that annoy you, or talk behind your back."

Chris affirms that our fallen humanness can come back with a vengeance and tempt us to go over the edge. And that's when we need to rely on God's power within us to make the right choice.

"There are times I'd like nothing more than to just blast people," she admits. "I used to do that. It used to feel good. But it doesn't anymore." Now it feels better, she says, when she pleases God first rather than herself.

By relying on God's power within her, Chris can react more carefully, in a Spirit-controlled manner, and save time in the long run. "I'd rather do it right the first time—in the beginning of a situation—rather than do something wrong and find it necessary to get it right the second time."

Today, Chris does not sound like a woman tormented by her past, but rather, one who is triumphing in her present: "Just because I had a mom who suffered from depression and mental turmoil doesn't mean I'm going to suffer from the same things," she told me. "No, I will *not* be just like my Mom. I'm going to take the good qualities from her that I want to emulate—her hospitality and her abilities as a homemaker—and leave the rest. I don't have to repeat the dysfunctional patterns of my past."

You don't have to either.

Retreat to a Spacious Place

Finally, Chris says she intentionally seeks out a "spacious place" regularly to keep from being on the edge. "I need to walk. I need to get outside and be by myself. I spend time in my garden. I love planting. I love color; I love seeing things grow."

Chris' garden is a place of solitude, a place of worship, a place of communing with God and praising Him for what He has done. I find it interesting that Chris loves planting seeds and watching plants grow. I believe that is symbolic of the planting and growing that God has allowed her to prompt in other people's lives...for His glory.

Living It Out

Although Chris may not see it for herself, she *is* very much like the noble wife described in Proverbs 31. She prioritizes her family, seeks to bless her husband and children—and nearly all who know her, for that matter—and her preferred place of influence is her home. She is others-focused and is the epitome of hospitality and grace. She loves being home in her kitchen whipping up a meal for her family, or in her garden admiring God's creation and cultivating the earth God put her on.

"I'm definitely a work in progress," Chris said humbly as she opened her Bible and read through verses 10-31 again, lining her life up to each verse. She laughed when she got to verse 16, which tells us the Proverbs 31 woman "considers a field and buys it; out of her earnings she plants a vineyard."

"I really want that vineyard someday," she said.

Chris does have a vineyard, however, and she has cultivated it carefully for years. The "fruit" in her vineyard include her two adult stepchildren, Cristina and Rico, whom she raised since they were 13 and 12 years old, respectively. Both are married now, are walking with the Lord, and are serving God in ministry. Her stepdaughter just gave birth to a baby girl, and is enjoying mirroring her stepmother's approach to honoring her family, her home, and her God. The other fruit in her vineyard, I believe, are the college-aged women, young moms, and other women who are drawn to her for spiritual growth and encouragement (I consider myself one of them!). Without realizing it, she has helped many women grow and bloom to their potential.

Reexamining the Lies

One of the reasons we sometimes feel we're about to go over the edge is that we believe we have no control over our lives and no ability to change dysfunctional patterns of the past. But the truth is, if we've surrendered our lives to Christ, *He* has the power to change us—from the inside out.

God's Word tells us He is able to do "immeasurably more than all we ask or imagine, according to his power that is at work within us" (Ephesians

3:20). In Ephesians 1:18-20, the apostle Paul prayed that we as Christians would know God's "incomparably great power" at work within us. The Greek word he used to speak of that kind of power is equivalent to our English words *hyper mega dynamite*. We refer to it as resurrection power. God's hyper mega dynamite power that He used to raise Christ from the dead can certainly raise you up from the things you think have a tight grip on you. That hyper mega dynamite power can break the chains on you from your past and give you a newfound life and freedom. *Hyper mega dynamite*—now that is power! And that is stronger than anything that threatens you from your past.

Take a look at some of the lies that real-life women on the edge struggle with and compare them with truths from God's Word:

> **Satan's Lie**: You will make the same mistakes your parents made.
>
> **God's Truth**: You are a *new creation* in Christ Jesus (2 Corinthians 5:17).

> **Satan's Lie**: You have never been loved.
>
> **God's Truth**: "I have loved you with an everlasting love" (Jeremiah 31:3).

> **Satan's Lie**: You have no future. You ought to just give it up now.
>
> **God's Truth**: "I know the plans I have for you...plans to give you hope and a future" (Jeremiah 29:11).

> **Satan's Lie**: God wants nothing to do with you.
>
> **God's Truth**: "God demonstrates his own love for us in this: While we were still sinners, Christ died for us" (Romans 5:8).

> **Satan's Lie**: God will never accept you or forgive you for what you have done.
>
> **God's Truth**: "Though your sins are like scarlet, they shall be as white as snow" (Isaiah 1:18).

A New Start

You can, tragically, believe the lies of Satan and let them destroy you. Or you can listen to the liberating truths of God's Word and let them transform you.

I believe it's time we let the truth put to rest the ticking that's supposedly going on inside of you and me. Why do we need to blow? Why do we need to sort through the damaged ways of our past? We have been cleaned up, redeemed, bought with a price, made new.

My friend, you don't need to run from your past or fear that you'll repeat it. You are new in Christ. Your past is erased. And because you have a God who promises to work all things for good to those who love God, you have a rich heritage, regardless of anything in your past. You have bitterness that He's turned to blessing, trials turned to treasure, and pain turned to purpose. That is redemption. And that is yours in a relationship with Christ, the Redeemer.

Returning to the Truth

I've known many a Christian woman who lived with the fear that the sins of her parents or grandparents or ancient ancestors had been—or would be—passed on to her and her children.

The idea that there might be such a thing as a generational curse is usually taken from Exodus 20:5, which says, "I, the Lord your God, am a jealous God, punishing the children for the sin of the fathers to the third and fourth generation of those who hate me."

Some people take this to mean that certain curses or sins can be *inherited* from parent to child. However, there is a major problem with accepting such a view. Deuteronomy 24:16 clearly states, "Fathers shall not be put to death for their children, nor children put to death for their fathers; each is to die for his own sin." That is, God punishes people for their own sins, not the sins of others. Ezekiel 18:2-20 affirms this as well, giving the example of a righteous father who "will surely live" (verse 9), yet his violent son "will surely be put to death" (verse 13). Then we read that the violent son happens to have a righteous son, and we are told the righteous son "will not die for his father's sin." The passage closes with this truth, "The soul who sins is the one who will die."

So the phrase "punishing the children for the sin of the fathers" in Exodus 20:5 cannot possibly refer to the idea of generational curses—that is, that God's punishment against one person will also be poured out upon the descendants of that person.

What, then, is Exodus 20:5 saying? It's not referring to children who have inherited sin from their parents, but rather to children who have *chosen to follow in the footsteps* of their parents. Children who choose to follow a pattern of sin established by their parents will be punished just as their fathers were punished. These children reveal their inclination by hating God just as their fathers hated God. But a child who breaks away from that sin pattern and chooses righteousness will be judged on the basis of his own choice, not his parents' behavior.

Another point Exodus 20:5 makes is that the effects of disobedience are powerful and can affect future generations. But later in that same verse we read that God shows "love to a thousand generations of those who love me and keep my commandments." In other words, the effects of obedience are even more powerful than the effects of disobedience.

Furthermore, God's Word tells us, "If anyone is in Christ he is a *new* creation; the old has gone, the new has come!"[19] *New creation*—did you catch that? There is no longer a link to your past. *Brand spanking new.* That's you when you are trusting in Christ's death as the penalty for your sin and His resurrection as your promise and inheritance of eternal life.

Do you realize that because of that promise in Scripture, you have within you more of a potential to be like Jesus than to be like your parents? The Holy Spirit working in you is more powerful than any past "generational sin" or deeply-ingrained habit or supposed genetic tendencies. In the words of theologian Lewis Sperry Chafer, "The new divine nature is more deeply implanted in your being than the human nature of your earthly father or mother."[20] That is reason to rejoice. You *are* free. And you are released from that pull from your past.

There are days when I, too, begin to fear I will follow in the footsteps of ancestors who walked in sin. (I can point to alcoholism, drug addiction, pride, legalism, homosexuality, adultery, and various obsessive compulsive disorders—on either or *both* sides of my family history.) And on the days when I hear the voice inside my head saying, "You will be just like that," it is then that I quote aloud the most liberating verse I know:

> I have been crucified with Christ; and it is no longer I who
> live, but Christ lives in me; and the life which I now live in

the flesh I live by faith in the Son of God, who loved me, and delivered Himself up for me (Galatians 2:20 NASB).

That verse reminds me that the old Cindi is dead and the new Cindi is Christ living in me. It reminds me that I am a new creation in Christ because of the blessed work of my Savior on the cross. And it reminds me I live by faith (and not by my own good efforts) in the One who loved me and gave Himself for me. What motivation! What inspiration! What liberation! So when thoughts come my way and tell me I can't avoid repeating patterns of the past, I remind myself that I am dead to the past and alive to Christ, who lives in and through me.

Did you catch that? Your sins, mistakes, and the dysfunctions from your past are *not* destined to grab hold of you and your children. The sins of the past will *not* follow you all the days of your life.

Rather, we are told in the final verse of Psalm 23, "Surely *goodness and love will follow me* all the days of my life, and I will dwell in the house of the LORD forever."[21]

As Christians, God's *goodness and love* is what *follows* us all the days of our lives. I don't believe that verse is saying we'll have God's goodness and love only in heaven after we die. It says "all the days of my life." And it says, "I will dwell in the house of the LORD forever." To dwell with God is to be living with Him now—not just someday. It means living in close communion with Him today—and every day. The Message renders that verse, "Your beauty and love chase after me every day of my life."

You, my friend, are not a dysfunctional woman-on-the-edge because of your past. You are a woman God *chases after* with love and goodness. Wow! Imagine how different your life would look if you truly believed that God's love and mercy follows you every day, rather than the sins that you feel you are so susceptible to. If you were to live in the awareness of God's mercy and love chasing after you, you'd be on the edge in a new, wondrous way. You'd be a woman living boldly, not timidly, for the One who redeemed you, regenerated you, and rushes after you with His love.

Finding Your Spacious Place

My eyes are ever on the LORD, for only he
will release my feet from the snare.

PSALM 25:15

Our fear of repeating the dysfunctional patterns of the past can cause us to live on the edge. So we must remember that our spacious place is who we are in God's eyes, and the fact that, through Christ's redemption, we have more of an ability to be like our heavenly Father than our earthly parents. Find your spacious place—and dwell there—by working through the application steps below.

1. What are some positive things you can remember about your upbringing that you would like to emulate?

2. What are the negatives you want no part of?

   Pray specifically that God would break these patterns from your past. Claim your new life in Christ and the power of His resurrection.

3. Memorizing Bible verses about your identity in Christ is key to living in your spacious place so you are no longer on the edge. Make it a personal challenge to memorize one or more of these verses as a reminder of who you are in Christ. Begin by writing out each of these verses below:

   2 Corinthians 5:17:

Galatians 2:20:

Romans 8:1:

Philippians 1:6:

4. Fill your name in the blanks and read this prayer aloud:

Thank You, heavenly Father, that I, _____, am a
new creation in Christ Jesus—that the old me and everything
associated with it is gone and the new me has come. Thank
You that I, _____, have been crucified with Christ
and it is no longer I who live, but Christ who lives in me and
the life I now live in the flesh I live by faith in the Son of God,
who loved me and gave Himself for me. Thank You that there
is no condemnation for _____, who is in Christ
Jesus. Because of this, I pray that I, _____, may
live a life worthy of the Lord and may please Him in every
way: bearing fruit in every good work, growing in the knowledge of God, being strengthened with all power according to
His glorious might so that I may have great endurance and
patience, and joyfully giving thanks to the Father, who has
qualified _____ to share in the inheritance of the
saints in the kingdom of light. For You have rescued me from
the dominion of darkness and brought me into the kingdom
of the Son You love, in whom _____ has redemption, the forgiveness of sins.[22]

For further reading and study on this topic, I recommend the following resources:

The Bondage Breaker by Neil Anderson, Harvest House Publishers

Victory over the Darkness by Neil Anderson, Regal Books

Lies Women Believe by Nancy Leigh DeMoss, Moody Publishers

Breaking Free by Beth Moore, LifeWay Christian Resources

7

Desperate to Accomplish

DESIRING HIM AS THE PRIZE

In his heart a man plans his course, but
the LORD determines his steps.

PROVERBS 16:9

C indy was a music artist on the edge. With a beautiful voice and a
musically talented husband at her side, she just needed her "big
break"—and a baby—for her life to be complete.

Six years after marrying, Cindy recorded her first CD. "I prayed that
God would open the doors for me to record my own CD. Michael [her
husband] told me that he had a friend in Nashville who had his own
recording studio. Michael's friend had an opening in the fall of 1998.
Everything fell into place."

But the baby Cindy and Michael longed for didn't fall into place quite
as quickly. After five more years of prayer and an operation to remove
a large benign polyp from Cindy's uterus, she finally became pregnant.
God had answered her and her husband's prayers with the birth of their
first son, Brian.

But there was still a self-imposed pressure on Cindy to "make it" in
the Christian world with her music. She was on the edge to keep using
the gift God had given her, even with a family at home. She was the
worship leader at her church, as well as for women's conferences locally
and a few overseas.

Then, within a couple of years after having their first child, their second son, Nathan was born—with Down syndrome. Suddenly, Cindy said, she was broken down and made to see what counts in life.

"I have been on my knees so much since Nathan was born," she said. "When you have a child with Down syndrome you can easily give in to fear when you think about the future. I had to take every thought captive under the obedience of Christ. It has made me need God every minute, with every breath."

The whirlwind of being a stay-at-home mom of two young children and trying to keep her music ministry going—while her husband traveled often for work—left Cindy even more frazzled and ready to go over the edge. That's when she put her ambitions on the altar and said, "God, I just want to accomplish Your will for my life. I want to be used by You in any way that You choose."

"I don't have that struggle to succeed anymore," Cindy told me recently over coffee. The once-frazzled woman had a sense of peace that I hadn't seen in her before. "I know now that our success is not based on how many people I know or how many people know my name, but on the lives I have impacted."

When Cindy surrendered her need to succeed and began to focus on glorifying God and serving others, God lifted her up and gave her more than she had originally asked. Her song "Lead Me," which she wrote and performed for the Gospel Music Association (GMA) became the runner-up in the GMA and American Bible Society Scripture Song Competition in 2008. Cindy realized that God had made a remarkable transformation in her life. It didn't matter to her if she became "famous" in the world's eyes or not. What mattered was that she was being faithful and obedient to the call that God had for her.

"People need to be touched by Jesus more than they need to be touched by me," she said. Cindy's ambition today? To know God more intimately and see *His* will accomplished in and through her life.

As Cindy looks back on her fierce determination to succeed with her music and what God has done in her life since then, she is able to say with confidence, "When we surrender our lives to God, He begins to change us into Christ's image—to make us more like Jesus. I believe God's desire for us is to die to ourselves completely. He uses different situations to bring us to the end of ourselves. And at the end of ourselves, God is there waiting to carry us through."

The Desires of Your Heart

What are *you* waiting for God to accomplish or "carry through" in your life?

We often quote Psalm 37:4 as our "guarantee" that God is going to come through with granting our desires. After all, that verse says, "Delight yourself in the LORD and he will give you the desires of your heart." We want *our* desires, and we want them *now*. But we need to look more closely at that verse and the one that follows. When God tells us to delight ourselves in Him, could it be that He is saying *when* we delight in Him, He will *place in us* certain desires that He will delight in granting? The verse that follows says, "Commit your way to the LORD, trust in him and he will do this" (verse 5). I believe God is saying, "Delight yourself in Me, and I will give you desires for what I desire, and then I'll gladly grant them."

Kristi, a 38-year-old mom in Georgia, is waiting on God for what she hopes to accomplish, too. "I have always wanted to be a songwriter. I have wondered why God put a desire in me but hasn't used me for that purpose, but I am learning that just like David waited twenty-two years for his promise to be fulfilled [to become Israel's king], so must I wait and enjoy the journey instead of just wishing I was at my destination."

Like Cindy, Kristi also had to wait on God to have children. "We tried for three years to get pregnant with no luck, and all my friends had children. I learned patience in a very real way, and learned a lot about depending on God's timing. I would like to believe that I offer hope to women who have or are going through the same thing. I now have beautiful twin boys, and I thank God every day for the blessings He has bestowed on me."

Kristi still doesn't have her songwriting career, but realizes that if God had a good and perfect reason for waiting when it came to giving her children, He must have a good and perfect reason for waiting in this matter of her life, as well.

If God has truly placed in Kristi the desire to write songs for Him, He will bring it about in His way and in His timing.

God's Wait-training

There are many stories in the Bible of people who waited for the fulfillment of a promise or the realization of a dream:

- Abraham waited 25 years for God to give him a promised son. His wife, Sarah, who was 65 at the time she heard the news, waited those 25 years, too! Talk about a woman on the edge! Yet God knew what He was doing in not letting Sarah have her baby until she was 90 years old. Think about it…God got a lot more glory for giving a 90-year-old barren woman a son than He would have if she had been 66!

- Moses, who probably believed he was ready to do great things for God in his twenties, had to wait *40 years* in the desert, herding sheep, before God raised him up to deliver His people out of Egypt. This man-on-the-edge who killed an Egyptian slave to protect a fellow Hebrew, still had some maturing to do before God would make him a national hero.

- David, the shepherd boy and giant-killer, waited 22 years to become king of Israel! The nation needed a leader like him long before he officially became king. But God was preparing this humble teenager in many ways to be a desperate man for Him before He let him sit on the throne.

Even my friend and recording artist Cindy, who waited five years to have a child—five years that seemed like an eternity—now sees that waiting as part of God's perfect timing.

"Because my parents died when I was a teenager, I had a lot of fears about having children of my own," she said. "I feared that if I had children, I might die and leave them. God had been working on my heart, helping to calm my fears. His timing is always perfect. In the waiting, He refines us and causes us to put our hope in Him, and not in whatever it is we're hoping to accomplish."

What have you been hoping to accomplish that God appears to be delaying?

My friend, Dawn Marie (whose story I told in chapter 5), knows well the experience of God withholding or delaying something for her own good. I already told you how God rescued her from a loveless marriage by having her seek Him first—and focus on *being* the right person rather than *finding* the right person. Then God gave her a husband a year later.

Now, as a talented writer and teacher of God's Word, Dawn Marie has been waiting on God for the past several years for her writing career. There doesn't appear to be a reason for the delay. Several months ago she told me, "Sometimes when I can't see how God is rearranging the details of my life to orchestrate a beautiful symphony of praise to His glory, I get hung up on the fact that, in my mind, some notes are missing. I have to trust Him, in those frustrating times, to reveal His will. He knows what He is doing, even when it is not obvious to me. I believe that in my mind. I have to remember to make choices based on that truth."

Dawn Marie waited on the Lord for His timing, and she has reaped the blessings of doing so. She has coauthored a devotional for teens with a friend who has been a writing mentor to her.[23] She is now working on a devotional of her own.

Can *you* wait for God's best when it comes to what *He* wants to accomplish through you? When we wait for His timing, we get what He has chosen for us, which is always far better and far more than what we get when we forge ahead and try to accomplish something on our own.

Have It *His* Way

Rhonda, an enthusiastic pastor's wife and vibrant Bible teacher in her late forties, is now waiting upon God to open the doors wider for speaking opportunities to women and to publish books.

"God has accomplished all that He has put in my heart to do up to this point," Rhonda told me recently. "However, there were times that God would whisper a desire to my heart, and make me long for and pray for that desire for long periods of time—as long as ten years—before He accomplished His plan."

Years ago, Rhonda and her husband went from youth ministry work and all of the camps and retreats and teaching opportunities to more adult ministries such as teaching women's studies, planning and speaking at events and retreats, and so on. "After I became quite busy every weekend, the Lord made it clear to my heart that if I continued to 'busy' myself with all of these engagements, I would risk 'losing' our youngest daughter, who was spending more and more time with friends each weekend, and being scooted away from my study as I prepared for the next event. In obedience, through tears, I resigned to minister first to her and told the Lord I would wait for His timing and not my own."

God honored Rhonda's willingness to lay her ambitions on the altar and desire God's will over hers. He honored her decision to please Him in the raising of her daughter, rather than run after what *she* had wanted at that time. And Rhonda did not regret honoring God, and seeing Him honor her, in return.

"Because I have not pursued being away at different teaching engagements, I have been able to fully minister to each of my children without neglecting to pour myself into their spiritual growth. God has still blessed me with many opportunities over the years to teach at youth and women's events, but I have not pursued them with the vengeance at which I had begun ten years ago."

As a result, Rhonda has been at her church most Sundays and available to mentor many of the women in her church in small discipleship groups as well as one-on-one. "I would have been too busy for these opportunities had I been on the go all of the time, always preparing for the next event that would take me away from my family and my ministry at my church."

Today, Rhonda is still speaking for women's groups, writing Bible studies, and waiting for God to open the door to book publishing. "I have personally always been amazed by the fact that God has a specific purpose planned out for my life. I have been in awe as I have watched Him unfold the life I have been blessed to live in ministry so far. I know that His plan for my next season of life will be orchestrated by Him as well, but living in the middle of 'Okay, Lord, what's next?' gets a little unclear." Yet Rhonda continues to trust the One who is paving the way before her…leading her to accomplish what *He* desires, in *His* time and in *His* way.

My Misdirected Dream

I remember being desperate to get my first book published. As a journalism major who had been writing all of my life, I knew *how* to write, but wasn't listening to God in terms of *what* to write. In fact, my dream was that my first book would have the title *Pathway to a Prince*, and that I would share how to find the perfect man. But as my book idea was turned down again and again, I eventually went to God and asked for two things: 1) that He would do the work necessary in my life to make me the kind of woman whose words other women would want to read; and 2) that He would show me His heart for women and what He wanted to say to them through me.

As I made those requests I remember thinking, *Who am I to think that God would use me to say anything to women?* He had humbled me in the process of making me wait and had moved me a long way from the thought, *Why is it taking God so long to help me accomplish my goals?* When we come to the Lord humbly and lay down our desires for His, He goes to work and makes us more like Him. And *then* He can use us in any way that He desires.

Over the next couple of years, God developed in me a heart for His Word and for prayer. What two better ways to get to know God and what is on *His* heart? During that time He also brought many women into my life for me to disciple and train in the Word of God. All the while, He was showing me my weaknesses and how He could meet them. So when I finally got published, my books resulted out of my personal studies of God's Word and where He could meet me—and the women I was discipling—if I surrendered completely to Him. God wanted me to write from the pain in my life so women could relate, not from the pride in my life so women could say, "I wish I had what she has!"

My first book, which was released ten years ago, was not *Pathway to a Prince.* It was, instead, *Letting God Meet Your Emotional Needs*—it was about how to surrender ourselves completely to Him and see Him meet the needs of our hearts. The next book was not *Pathway to a Prince,* either. It was *When Women Walk Alone,* about how God draws us closer to Himself during our alone times. Suffice it to say, none of my books have been the one I originally thought I'd write. But all of them have, in a sense, paved a path toward the Prince who brings us joy, rest, and fulfillment when we surrender our lives to Him.

God's Way Over Mine

God's way and timing are always going to be so much better than ours because He is able to do "immeasurably more than all we ask or imagine, according to his power that is at work within us" (Ephesians 3:20).

As we strive for accomplishment, God's Word tells us that our "success" in this life is clearly in His hands. Look at what God has to say when it comes to *our* ambitions:

1. *God wants us to seek His kingdom first.* Matthew 6:33 says, "Seek first His kingdom and his righteousness, and all these things [that you want to accomplish] will be given to you as well."

2. *God wants us to be completely His; then He will support our desires.* "The eyes of the LORD move to and fro throughout the earth that he may strongly support those whose heart is completely His" (2 Chronicles 16:9 NASB).

3. *God is the One who "markets" us and promotes our efforts.* "Promotion cometh neither from the east, nor from the west, nor from the south. But God is the judge; he putteth down one, and setteth up another" (Psalm 75:6 KJV).

4. *God's ways are bigger and better than ours.* Isaiah 55:8-9 says, "'My thoughts are not your thoughts, neither are your ways my ways,' declares the LORD. 'As the heavens are higher than the earth, so are my ways higher than your ways and my thoughts than your thoughts.'" That means we shouldn't try to outguess or outperform God. If He says wait, we need to wait. If He says, "Do it differently," we need to listen.

5. *God's goal is that we become more like His Son.* We often quote Romans 8:28 because we like the fact that "in all things God works for the good of those who love him." But we forget the qualifying statement in verse 29, which explains *why* He does that: "For those God foreknew he also predestined to be conformed to the likeness of his Son..." It's our transformation into the likeness of Jesus' character that God is concerned about. So if our dreams and ambitions don't match His, He will intervene with something that will make us more like Him. And if we aren't able to accomplish something as soon as we would like, God will use that time to make us more like His Son.

It sounds like God is more concerned about what we become in the process of trying to accomplish something than about what we actually accomplish. It's ironic that while we get frustrated when we feel we *can't* accomplish a certain work, that's when God *can* accomplish His intended work in *us*.

A Song of Surrender

So where does that leave us? If we aren't able to accomplish that which is burning on our hearts, are we to remain on the edge and blame God for it? We could, I suppose. But that wouldn't get us anywhere. He knows the plans He has for us, and He will bring them about when we are ready to surrender our lives to Him and say, as Jesus did in Luke 22:42, "Not my will, but yours be done." As we surrender our "to do" list to Him, He gives us His, and He equips us with all we will need to accomplish those things for His glory. Then, at the end of our lives, we can say, as Jesus did in one of His last prayers on earth, "I have brought you glory on earth by completing the work you gave me to do" (John 17:4).

Oh, how I want to say that when I meet Jesus face-to-face someday, don't you? I want to say it so much that it gives me an edge for wanting to get it done and get it done right for Him. Can you have that kind of an edge, too? Can you possess a passion to see God accomplish much in your life while you still have breath?

As Cindy told me recently, "It's a choice we all have to make—to follow God's plan and yield to Him, or to follow our own desires."

As God was working those lessons in Cindy's life, she penned her song of surrender (which became an award-winning song I mentioned earlier). Pray through these words and see if you can make this *your* song of surrender as well:

Just to sit at Your feet
Just to say, "I give You all of me"
Oh Lord, I long to be with You

And everything I am
I surrender to Your plan
I trust You, Lord and I'll follow where You lead

(Chorus)
So lead me to greener pastures
Sweeter songs, happy ever afters
I'll believe Your promises for me

So lead me beside still waters, where I long to be
You're the Shepherd of my life, so lead me

(Verse 2)
And everything I'm going through
Lord, I give it all to You
I will rest in the shadow of Your wings

For I know Your plans for me
Are for hope and life and peace
I will trust You Lord, and I'll follow where You lead

(Chorus)

(Bridge)
And though this road may seem so long
I hear You calling out my name
And I will follow close behind
For You're showing me the way[24]

What's *Your* Song?

Can you sing of the One whose ambition is to make you more like Himself? Can you look at all you want to accomplish in your life and run it through the grid of what He ultimately wants for your life? If it is Him you seek and His glory that you long for, your desires and dreams will glorify Him and He will be pleased to accomplish them in and through you. You don't have to be on the edge any longer in what you want to accomplish. Just get that edge for Him, and He will take care of the rest.

Finding Your Spacious Place

You, LORD, are all I want!
You are my choice, and you keep me safe.
You make my life pleasant, and my future is bright.

PSALM 16:5-6 CEV

Our drive to accomplish can take us over the edge if we are not careful to bring our desires to God and ask for His will, His way, and His timing. When He becomes our greatest prize, He will delight in granting to us our heart's desire. Work through the following applications to make sure *He* is the prize you are seeking.

1. What one or two things would you like to accomplish before you die?

2. Now think in terms of a legacy, not a mere accomplishment. How do you want to be remembered after you're gone by those closest to you?

3. How are your goal and your legacy connected?

4. Read the following verses. You may want to try reading them in a few different translations. What does each verse say about God's desire for your life?

Romans 8:29:

Ephesians 2:10:

Ephesians 3:16-19:

5. Pray through Psalm 18:25-36 and surrender to God what it is you're desperate to accomplish. Keep in mind that if it's His desire, He will bring it about.

For further encouragement and direction in this area, I recommend the following resources:

When a Woman Discovers Her Dream by Cindi Mc-Menamin, Harvest House Publishers

The Dream Giver by Bruce Wilkinson, Multnomah Publishers

8

Desperate to Find Yourself

DESIRING HIS IDENTITY OVER YOURS

Whoever finds his life will lose it, and whoever
loses his life for my sake will find it.

JESUS, MATTHEW 10:39

Belinda looked straight into my eyes as she explained why she left her husband of 25 years: "I married when I was 17 years old. I didn't have an identity. I didn't even know who I was."

After a season of discovering many things about herself—that she was artistic, she loved people, she had a servant's heart and enjoyed taking care of others—she also realized she was a woman who loved God and wanted to be obedient to Him. She knew that meant not deserting her marriage vows. She returned to her marriage after a six-month separation and, 20 years later, is not regretting her decision to trust God with who *He* is—someone who would honor her if she held tight to her situation and trusted Him over her own confusion about who she might or might not be.

Angelique sat on the floor of her one-bedroom apartment, ready to take her life. The frustrated single mother of a 9-year-old daughter was tired of grappling with her unanswered questions: *Who am I? Why am I here? Does anyone really care?*

As she was contemplating how she would end her life that evening, her thoughts were interrupted by a knock on the door. When she opened it, there stood two women from her church. They handed her a book called

When Women Walk Alone[25] and said: "We thought of you this evening while we were in a group study of this book. We wanted you to have this. And we'd love for you to join us next week."

After they left, Angelique opened the book and started reading. By the time she got to the end of the first chapter, she was in tears on her knees at the edge of her bed, where she gave her life to Christ.

"It never, ever occurred to me that there might actually be a reason for the pain I've had in my life," she told me several months later. "When I realized God wanted to draw me closer to Him through my aloneness, it changed my life and made me want to live again."

Instead of continuing to search for herself, Angelique began to search for God. And in finding Him, she found her reason for living and a sense of who she was in *His* sight.

Helen was truly a woman on the edge. She married right out of high school to a man she hardly knew. She then spent much of her married life searching for her identity, striving for peace in a stormy marriage, and struggling to keep her sanity while raising three young children. By the time her children reached high school, she divorced her husband, whom she claimed "never really knew me," married an old boyfriend from high school "who has always thought the world of me," and moved on, claiming she had finally found herself. But today, at nearly 60 years old, she is divorced again, her children are estranged from her, and she continues to wonder if she is on the right path for her life.

What is at the root of our search for identity? Why are we so consumed with trying to "find" ourselves? Is there really a piece of us missing out there that we must find? I believe that rather than needing to *find* ourselves, we need to *forget* about ourselves and focus on the One who created us to love Him and enjoy Him forever. I truly believe our struggle to find ourselves, our search for our identity, reflects an ignorance of who we are in the eyes of our Creator, how much we're worth in the eyes of our Redeemer, and the extent of our ability to glorify Him simply by loving and living for Him.

As you read Kelly's story, you may come to understand what causes us to search for significance—a search that can put us on the path toward destruction rather than the path that leads toward life.

Kelly's Search for Significance

Kelly grew up content and happy, with no real issues at home. It was her search for significance, however—her desperation to find herself—that led her down a dark path of eating disorders that threatened to take her life. Because Kelly's condition could grab a hold of any one of us without us even realizing it, I will let her tell you her story in her own words:

> I was always very active in sports and cheerleading, joining about every social club I could think of. I found myself to be a very fast runner, which sort of became my identity. I was the League MVP as a freshman and enjoyed all the glory that came with that. I knew who I was…a cheerleader, a runner, a social girl with lots of friends. I liked attention, as most high school kids do. I so desired to be popular and well liked.
>
> Then one day at a cheerleading competition during my senior year, when I was doing the tumbling part of a routine, I slipped and fell. I jumped up and continued, but I was never the same. I had broken some bones in my ankle. I was faced with endless doctor visits and an end to my track career. I had hoped to get a scholarship and run in college, but not anymore. All those changes began to scare me. *Who was I? If running was my identity and it was why people liked me, what would happen if that was taken away?*
>
> I really began to be afraid. I also feared that I would begin to gain weight because, for the first time in my life, I wasn't active. So I began to diet. At first that was probably very normal for a girl my age, but soon I became obsessive. I started to lose a lot of weight and gain attention from my family and friends—attention that I desired so much.
>
> Long story short, that dieting spiraled toward a downhill path of full-blown eating disorders. When I graduated from high school, I had no idea what to do. There were a lot of changes ahead of me, and I now believe it was those changes that God used to draw me to Christ. I felt like the rug was being

yanked out from under me, and that's when Jesus stepped in to catch me! A few friends of mine had been sharing the gospel with me, and I had been ignoring them. I started to listen, and finally, in June of 1979, one week after I graduated, I accepted Christ into my heart.

When August came, I moved away and went to a college a few hours from my home. Although I was now a believer, I didn't know that I should get into a Bible study or begin to read the Word of God. I knew I was different on the inside, but I didn't know what to do about it on the outside. So I continued in the same lifestyle. My eating disorders got worse and worse. I didn't realize I could call on the Lord for help. I just figured I could "fix" this problem; I could get over this all by myself.

I sank deeper and deeper into a black prison of endless cycles of eating and throwing up, or starving myself. I bounced from anorexia to bulimia. No one knew how to help me. I told everyone I was fine. I even fooled some people. But I never fooled God. I was depressed, discouraged, and distraught. I really did want help, but knew if I asked for it, I would be made to eat, so I couldn't risk it. I felt like I was looking at the world through prison bars, watching the happy people around me live their lives and dreaming that I could be one of them someday. That didn't even seem to stem from a desire to be liked, or a desire for attention and identity. Rather, I felt as if I were in bondage, as if a glove were tightly wrapped around me.

I moved back home to have an operation on my foot. There, I began attending a local Bible-believing church. The pastor always read from the Bible, and even encouraged us to read it for ourselves. I was being drenched in the Word of God. I couldn't get enough; I was there every time they opened the doors. I began to understand who God was, what sin was, and how a holy God viewed ugly sin.

And one day, in my bedroom, the Holy Spirit directed me to Psalm 51. It's the psalm that tells the response of King David when the prophet Nathan confronted David about his secret sin with Bathsheba, saying, "You are the man!"[26] David was found out! He said in verse 3-4, "I know my transgressions, and my sin is always before me. Against you, you only, have I sinned and done what is evil in your sight."

David had come to realize how greatly his sin had grieved the heart of God. And it was at that moment that I realized that what I was doing was sin. My body, my self, had become my idol. I was in control of my life, not God. Every time I chose to abstain from food, or throw up, or whatever, I was sinning against God, and was breaking His heart.

That day I finally, truly surrendered my life to Him. I gave Him control of everything. I understood at last the depth of my sin. I cried out to God for forgiveness, and for strength to help me overcome this addiction. He forgave me that night. He gave me strength to fight the battle against my addiction. It was a struggle to make the right choices, but God helped me every step of the way. It was a long, upward climb, but God did it. Jesus delivered me from darkness and despair into His glorious light, and I am forever grateful for that!

Delivered and Directed

After Kelly was delivered from her eating disorders, she realized she had also been delivered from her desperate search to find herself. She doesn't need to be "thin" to know who she is. She doesn't need to be "in control" to know who she is. As she focuses on the One who loves her, she knows she is loved. As she focuses on the One who is all-powerful, she knows she can do all things through Christ. As she focuses on the One who has purchased her with a price,[27] she knows she is of great value. As she seeks more of Him, she finds more of life to the full.

"Although this world brings many difficult trials and challenges, we look to Him for the answers," Kelly says. "We look to Him for our security. We look to Him for hope because He has promised us a heavenly home, a place prepared for us. If I can keep my eyes focused on Him, and cling to Him, for He is my life, then all will be well. It's not easy, simple, or fun. But it will be well with my soul. He broke down the prison walls and set me free. And I am free indeed!"

Today, Kelly no longer desires to find herself. Rather, she longs to know God in a deeper way, and as a result, she has come to see who she is in His sight. Her desperation for a sense of identity nearly led her to self-destruction. But her desperation to show God how grateful she is for what He's done for her has led her to a life that is liberating and a ministry that is life-changing.

Kelly, who is now in her late forties, has been a pastor's wife for nearly 25 years and serves alongside her husband in his church, where she is the director of women's ministries. She blesses women through the countless Bible studies she has written and taught and the conference speaking she continues to do.

"I have always felt horrible about the fact I wasted so much time serving myself and my desires," she says. "So years ago [on the night she rededicated her life to Christ], I told the Lord that I wanted to serve Him every day of my life! He gave me Matthew 22:37 as my life verse: 'You shall love the Lord your God with all your heart, and with all your soul, and with all your mind' [NASB]. I chose that verse not because I've attained it, but because it's my goal—to learn how to love Him more and more every day.

"I have a passion to teach women of all ages about how much God loves them—about how their identity should be wrapped up in Christ. I want them to know that being in control of themselves and living lives of selfishness and pride is the root of almost every sin, and it will end in destruction. The enemy of our souls pursues us relentlessly, and we can't believe the lies the world tells us about our self-worth."

What Are *You* Searching For?

As you read Kelly's story, you may think, *I would never resort to an eating disorder.* Yet studies show one in five women struggle from an eating disorder or disordered eating.[28] And nearly half of all Americans personally know someone who has an eating disorder.[29]

The desperation for significance manifests itself in many subtle yet self-destructive ways. Sometimes it manifests itself in obsessive behavior or addictions. Because we can end up on the destructive path of trying to find ourselves without even realizing it, here are a few of the symptoms:

Do you ever find yourself...

- continually searching for your significance? Are you constantly agitated over not knowing your purpose or special niche? Are you known to have one hobby or interest after another, none of which lasts longer than a year or two?

- obsessing about your age? Are you aggravated by thoughts that your life might be half over, that there are still so many things you haven't done with your life, that you're no longer able to do (or wear) certain things, that you have more wrinkles and rolls on your body and less muscle, energy, and vigor?

- obsessing about your weight? Do you think, several times throughout the day, about what you're eating, whether or not you should eat, how much you've eaten, or what you weigh? Or, are you constantly thinking about exercise, your heart rate, the number of steps you've taken, or your daily caloric burn?

- obsessing about your looks? Do you fantasize about having plastic surgery, fitting into a smaller-size dress, having a smaller waist or nose, having larger lips, or having a different bust?

When we are consumed with thoughts about ourselves, we are headed toward self-destruction. But when we are consumed with thoughts of God, our lives will look completely different. Think about it: An addict is one who will do *anything*—even if it is immoral, illegal or unethical—to get her fix. When you are obsessed with God, on the other hand, you are willing to do anything to have Him, please Him, or sense His presence. When you are consumed with Christ, your identity becomes wrapped up in His, and as a result, you will become more like Him.

Survival Steps for an Identity Crisis

When it comes to eating disorders, Kelly can still be tempted by the enemy to return to her old ways. She is still taunted, at times, that her significance lies in how she looks or what she weighs. And no matter what our area of weakness, no matter what our age or stage in life, you and I can be tempted to go down a self-destructive path as well.

To help you steer clear of that path, Kelly helped me come up with what I call Survival Steps for an Identity Crisis. These are useful toward both current or future crises.

1. Ignore the Lies and Invest in the Truth

You will have days when your negative self-talk tells you that you are worthless. You'll have days when the enemy of your soul will torment you with thoughts that you're not young enough, thin enough, or attractive enough to experience real happiness in life. You'll have days when the enemy will taunt you to start walking a path toward your own identity. But beware: Christ told us to lose our life (quit focusing on ourselves) in order to find it. When you look at yourself, you will see your short-comings, weaknesses, and mistakes. But when you direct your gaze at Christ, you will find perfection, strength, unconditional love, beauty, and completeness.

"Satan is a liar, and all his tricks are full of deception," Kelly instructs. "So I combat his lies with the belt of truth and the sword of the Spirit. I remind myself first of what God's Word tells me about significance, and love, and what's important to Him. I also remind myself about the things my husband and friends tell me [about the truth of how she looks], what size I wear, and so on. I just keep going back to the truth. Then I ask the Lord to help me hold onto that, get my focus on Him, and bind the enemy from my thoughts." Kelly makes a practice of applying 2 Corinthians 10:5:

> We demolish arguments and every pretension that sets itself up against the knowledge of God, and we take captive every thought to make it obedient to Christ.

2. Immerse Yourself in God's Word

Reciting Scripture helps keep our minds focused on God's truth rather than Satan's lies. The Word also keeps us unstained by the world and its ideals, philosophies, and values. The world will tell you—on television, the radio, in songs, across the table at the coffee shop—that you are the most important person in your life and finding yourself is paramount. But Jesus said, "If your first concern is to look after yourself, you'll never find yourself. But if you forget about yourself and look to me, you'll find both yourself and me" (Matthew 10:39 MSG).

Kelly begins her day at a coffee shop, where she immerses herself in God's Word to keep His truth—instead of the world's lies—at the forefront of her mind.

3. Invite Accountability into Your Life

Kelly says, "If I'm really struggling, I ask a friend for prayer. While it's sort of embarrassing to admit I need help with even the little things in life, it helps to get those things out in the open. Proverbs 27:17 tells us that as iron sharpens iron, so one man or woman sharpens another." The Bible also tells us of the benefit of having another person in our life who can hold us accountable and keep us from falling:

> Two are better than one,
>> because they have a good return for their work:
> If one falls down,
>> his friend can help him up.
> But pity the man who falls
>> and has no one to help him up!...
> Though one may be overpowered,
>> two can defend themselves.
> A cord of three strands is not quickly broken
>> (Ecclesiastes 4:9-10,12).

4. Incorporate Daily Prayer into Your Life

If you pray only when you're in trouble, then you're in trouble. Prayer keeps us focused on God. It needs to be continual so we don't lose our focus and start thinking of ourselves again. First Thessalonians 5:17 tells us to "pray continually." In that way, we can keep our focus more on God than on ourselves. When we struggle with feelings of guilt or shame, with wanting to feel more significant, or with wanting something in our life to change, we need to redirect our focus onto God and start praising Him. When we recount God's goodness, recite His faithfulness, and repeat songs of His worthiness, it helps move our attention from our self pity to our Savior's praise. We see this principle affirmed in the Psalms: The songwriters start out *on their faces in pity*. Then they get *on their knees in prayer*. Then, as they turn their gaze toward God, they are able to get up *on their feet in praise*.

To see this in action, consider David in Psalm 13:

> How long, O LORD? Will you forget me forever?
> How long will you hide your face from me?

How long must I wrestle with my thoughts
and every day have sorrow in my heart?...
[*That's David on his face in pity.*]
Look on me and answer, O LORD my God.
Give light to my eyes or I will sleep in death...
[*That's David on his knees in prayer.*]
But I trust in your unfailing love;
my heart rejoices in your salvation.
I will sing to the LORD,
for he has been good to me.
[*That's David on his feet in praise!*]
(Psalm 13:1-2,3,5)

The Song at the End of the Search

Read through Kelly's words of praise, in which she declares she now sees her significance in God, and not in anything in and of herself. Her path is now one of life:

He is the answer; He is my Deliverer; My Redeemer that had redeemed the years I let the locust eat; He is my song, because I didn't have one. He is my Freedom because I was in bondage; He is my Strength because He is what keeps me going and not "falling off the edge." He is my wisdom because He shows me how and where to walk. He is my true love, because He loves me just as I am. And He is my life... because I sincerely believe I would have lost mine...I was headed down the path of destruction.

Can you also proclaim the goodness of the One who is the Answer at the end of your search? Can you praise the One who is the Healer of your hurts and the Redeemer of your wasted years of looking in the wrong direction for hope and happiness? Will you, in this moment, surrender your search for yourself and replace it with the realization that you have found all you could ever want? There is something wonderful in being able to say, "I've finally found what I've been looking for!"

Finding Your Spacious Place

Obsession with self...is a dead end;
attention to God leads us out into the open,
into a spacious, free life.

ROMANS 8:5 MSG

If we continue to search for significance within ourselves, our search will come up empty. But as we search the Scriptures to see who we are in God's eyes, we realize we have worth, purpose, and a glorious inheritance if we are trusting Jesus Christ for our salvation. Go through the following exercises as a refresher course of who you are in God's eyes.

1. Read the following passages and record what each one says about your identity in God's eyes:

   Psalm 139:13-16:

   Matthew 6:26:

   Ephesians 1:3-14:

2. Using Psalm 13 as a guide, fill in the blanks below and write your own "song" to the Lord regarding your personal search for identity:

   How long, O Lord? Will you forget me forever? How long will I _____?

How long must I wrestle with _____
and every day have sorrow in my heart?

How long will _____ get
the best of me?

Look on me and answer, O Lord my God. Give light to my
eyes so I can _____
_____.

I trust in your unfailing love; my heart rejoices in your salvation. I will sing to the Lord, for He has _____
_____.

Signed _____

Date _____

(Sign and date your song as a commitment to look to the Lord
for your identity.)

Part Two

Thriving on the Edge

DESPERATIONS THAT CAN LIBERATE

We've looked at desperations that can devastate if they
are not redirected toward God and what He desires of
us. Now let's look at the few desperations in life that can
truly liberate as we make them a driving force in our lives.

Continue with me on this journey as we look at being
desperate to obey Him, desperate to serve Him, desperate
for His life-giving touch, and desperate to glorify Him.

Desperate to Obey Him

DESIRING HIS WILL OVER YOURS

Direct my footsteps according to your word;
let no sin rule over me.

PSALM 119:133

I sat across the table from PJ. She looked desperate. "I don't know why I keep doing the things I'm doing," she vented. "I never used to sin in certain ways. Yet now, for the stupidest reasons, I will. I get irritated with people around me and I really don't have reason for it. I keep blowing it. There's something going on inside of me."

PJ was raised with a belief in God, but never knew what it meant to surrender her life to Jesus Christ until a few months ago. We were meeting weekly for discipleship and she was learning quickly what it means to have a relationship with Christ and grasping spiritual truths beyond her years. She had experienced great days of victory. But she was beginning to go through some depressing days of defeat—days in which she felt immense regret and shame for not being obedient to her Lord.

"I'm the epitome of hypocrisy," PJ told me one day at lunch. I told her that regrettably we *all* are, at one time or another.

PJ was experiencing the struggle that every one of us face after we have surrendered our lives to God—that struggle in which our human flesh rears its ugly head and tries to suppress our new nature, which belongs to Christ. It's the age-old battle between the flesh and the spirit—we want to live right but don't attain it; we strive to be obedient but we fall short. That battle can set us on edge.

I admitted to PJ that even though I had a relationship with God for longer than she had, I too still faced that struggle. Though we are new creatures in Christ, we still struggle in our fallen bodies of flesh. Not until we receive our resurrection bodies will that change.

I told PJ I never wanted to hear that she no longer struggled, or that she didn't notice the struggle anymore. Sure, it would be great if we never struggled at all to obey God and we became perfect such that we simply weren't tempted anymore. But the apostle Paul—one of Christ's most devoted followers and the writer of much of the New Testament—told us toward the *end* of his life that even he still battled against his flesh. None of us will know freedom from that struggle until the day we die.

That Seemingly Uncrossable Chasm

I came across a prayer in my devotional reading that so described the edge I feel at times—that frustration of not being who I truly desire to be, and yet wondering if I ever will be.

> O Lord Jesus Christ, Son of the living God, have mercy on me, a sinner. I am impressed by my own spiritual insights... I have read many books about the Christian life, and have even written a few myself. Still, as impressed as I am, I am more impressed by the enormous abyss between my insights and my life.
>
> It seems as if I am standing on one side of a huge canyon and see how I should grow toward you, live in your presence and serve you, but cannot reach the other side of the canyon where you are. I can speak and write, preach and argue about the beauty and goodness of the life I see on the other side, but how, O Lord, can I get there? Sometimes I even have the painful feeling that the clearer the vision, the more aware I am of the depth of the canyon.
>
> Am I doomed to die on the wrong side of the abyss? Am I destined to excite others to reach the promised land while remaining unable to enter there myself?...You alone, Lord, can reach out to me and save me. You alone.[30]

When I saw how another author described so perfectly the struggles I face, I wondered if perhaps the more we desire to be obedient, the more we become aware of the times when we aren't. And could it be that the more we desire to cross the chasm that divides us from where we want to be, the more distant and uncrossable the chasm appears?

The Battle That Rages Within

I'm so glad the apostle Paul was vulnerable and honest about the struggles within him when he wrote to the Christians in Rome. Paul's words of encouragement to those new Christians says something of his humility, as well as his desperation to be obedient to Christ:

> I know that nothing good lives in me, that is, in my sinful nature. For I have the desire to do what is good, but I cannot carry it out. For what I do is not the good I want to do; no, the evil I do not want to do—this I keep on doing...What a wretched man I am! Who will rescue me from this body of death? (Romans 7:18-19,24).

Now if Paul's letter to the Roman Christians had ended there, we would all be quite depressed, feeling no hope whatsoever. "What a wretched man I am!" Paul exclaimed. And like me, you might find yourself echoing Paul's exclamation ("What a wretched woman I am!") and his seemingly hopeless question, "Who will set me free from this body of death?" But the glorious answer is right there for us to rejoice in: "Thank God! The answer is in Jesus Christ our Lord" (Romans 7:25 NLT).

Paul then goes on to give us hope in the midst of that battle that rages within:

> There is no condemnation for those who belong to Christ Jesus. And because you belong to him, the power of the life-giving Spirit has freed you from the power of sin that leads to death. The law of Moses was unable to save us because of the weakness of our sinful nature. So God did what the law could not do. He sent his own Son in a human body like the bodies we sinners have. And in that body God declared an end to sin's control over us by giving his Son as sacrifice for our sins. He did this so that the just requirement of the law would be fully satisfied for us, who no longer follow our sinful nature but instead follow the Spirit (Romans 8:1-4 NLT).

That is our song of liberty. As wretched as we may feel at times because we continue to struggle with sin, we are not condemned for it because those who are trusting Christ Jesus for forgiveness have no condemnation. He took the shame. He bore the pain. He chose the nails. In exchange, He hands us life. And we are no longer slaves to sin, but rather, we are set free from a life of continual disobedience.

> Thanks be to God that, though you used to be slaves to sin, you wholeheartedly obeyed the form of teaching to which you were entrusted. You have been set free from sin and have become slaves to righteousness (Romans 6:17-18).

Living in Obedience

So how do we live like one who is no longer a slave to sin? How do we live by the power of the life-giving Spirit that has freed us from the power of sin? How do PJ and you and I claim victory over the old life of sin and live in the new nature of righteousness that we've been given?

Let Go of Self

Scripture tells us to die to self; reject the ways of the old nature and live according to the new nature. I remember, as a teenager, being told that whatever nature we feed is the nature that will grow and dominate the other. "Don't feed the monster" we would say to each other in my youth group as I was growing up. The monster of self is fed when we give it what it wants. But if we deny self, thereby starving it of what it wants, it tends to go dormant and the Spirit can dominate. Let go of self by refusing to feed it. Feed, instead, the Spirit through prayer, reflection on God's Word, and filling your mind with life-giving matters rather than the things that lead to disobedience and death.

Live Under the Spirit's Control

We are either controlled by our flesh or by the Spirit of God. To be filled—or controlled—by the Holy Spirit, we must continually yield to Him and die to ourselves. We know we are yielding to the Spirit when our lives produce the results (or fruit) of the Spirit. In Galatians 5:22-23, we are given a list of the characteristics that become evident in our lives when we yield control daily to the Spirit of God: "The fruit of the Spirit is love, joy, peace, patience, kindness, goodness, faithfulness, gentleness and self-control."

Look through that list. Those characteristics don't describe a woman on the edge, do they? One day when I was feeling out of sorts, I wrote out the opposite of what that verse is saying:

> The result of a life controlled by me is a critical nature, negativity, anxiety, impatience, cruelty, rudeness, a preoccupation with my own interests, brashness, and impulsive outbursts of anger.

When I saw, in horror, that those words described me that day, I realized I was certainly not living like a woman who was under the Spirit's control. The characteristics sounded more like a woman about to go over the edge because she was trying to get through life without yielding to the power of God's Spirit. I confessed the ugliness in my heart and asked God to put to death the results of a life lived under my own control and fill me anew with His Spirit, His characteristics, His life.

Love One Another

Loving others is possible when we let go of self, and live under the Spirit's control. As we saw in chapter 5, Jesus said that if we love Him, we will obey His commands. Five times He said that in one sitting. And then He commanded that we love one another. To love God first, then others, then ourselves is to put our faith into action and live obediently.

A True Desperation for God

But is obeying God enough? We can be like other women who call themselves followers of Christ and simply obey. But this book is not about mere obedience. It's about being on the edge for God. It's about not being satisfied with the status quo. It's about developing a true desperation for God. So let's talk about raising the bar, getting God's attention, and going above and beyond. You may be thinking, *But wait. How can we raise the bar? It is only by God's grace that we can receive any merit with Him.*

That's true. Yet in the Old Testament we read of a prophet, Hanani, who came to King Asa of Judah and told the king he was being punished because he relied on another king for his security rather than relying on the Lord. Hanani's words to this king imply that God constantly searches for hearts that are not only obedient, but fully committed to Him:

The eyes of the Lord move to and fro throughout the earth
that He may strongly support those whose heart is completely
His (2 Chronicles 16:9 NASB).

In other words, God is searching for a few good hearts—not because
He only *wants* a few, but probably because He can only *find* a few that
are truly committed, truly desperate to obey Him. Imagine that! God
searches the world for people whose hearts are so in tune with loving Him
and wanting to please Him that when He finds them, He takes notice
and "strengthens"[31] them, or shows Himself strong on their behalf.[32]

We see a *few good hearts* in Scripture—people whom God singled out
for being fully committed to Him:

- God singled out Moses to lead the Israelites out of bondage.
  During that time, God called Moses up to Mount Sinai to be
  with Him for 40 days[33] and spoke "face to face" with Moses "as
  a man speaks with his friend."[34] Later, God personally buried
  Moses' 120-year-old body when he died.[35] Moses is the only
  person Scripture describes as one "whom the LORD knew face
  to face" (Deuteronomy 34:10).

- God singled out Abraham to bless him and build a nation for
  him. God also called Abraham His "friend" (2 Chronicles
  20:7; Isaiah 41:8; James 2:23).

- God singled out Mary of Nazareth to become the mother of
  the Messiah. Through the angel Gabriel, God called Mary
  "highly favored" (Luke 1:28).

- And God referred to David—the shepherd boy, psalmist, and
  favorite king of Israel—as "a man after his own heart" (1 Samuel
  13:14; see also Acts 13:22).

Moses, Abraham, Mary, and David were all desperate for God. And
as 2 Chronicles 16:9 says, God supports those whose hearts are completely
His. Again, God said, "I have found David the son of Jesse, a man after
My own heart, who *will do all My will*" (Acts 13:22 NKJV).

There it is—David's distinction and why God singled him out—He
was willing to do *all* of God's will. David wasn't content with obeying

most of God's will. He wanted to be *completely* His. He was one who pursued not only obedience, but God's pleasure.

We see more of David's heart in the songs he wrote. In the first line of Psalm 15, David says, "LORD, who may dwell in your sanctuary? Who may live on your holy hill?" David was basically asking a question we've all wondered about: "Who can get close to You, God? Who can be Your best friend?" David then answered his question by creating a profile of what God's friend would look like:

> Only those who obey God and do as they should.
> They speak the truth and don't spread gossip;
> > They treat others fairly and don't say cruel things.
> They hate worthless people,
> > but show respect for all who worship the LORD.
> And they keep their promises, no matter what the cost.
> They lend their money without charging interest,
> > and they don't take bribes to hurt the innocent.
> Those who do these things will always stand firm
> > (Psalm 15:2-5 CEV).

A closer look at this description shows that David is not just talking about actions, but a lifestyle, a character. Our actions will not make God love us any more than He already does. But a life committed to obedience *will* place us in a position where God will draw nearer to us.[36] God is looking not only for obedience, but for a lifestyle of humility and holiness.

Leaving a Legacy

It's interesting that the apostle Paul's description of David was the same description God used for David when He anointed the shepherd boy king of Israel. That tells us that, centuries later, God's legacy for David was that he was still a man who had pursued God with all his heart. That is encouraging to me because—if you look at the life of David in the Scriptures—you will see he committed some heinous sins. In 2 Samuel 11 we read of a dark season in David's life when he lusted after a married woman, brought her into his bedroom while her husband was out fighting in a war, slept with her and caused her to conceive a child, then tried to cover up his fault by bringing her husband home from war to sleep with her and eventually believe she was pregnant with *his*—not David's—child. When that plan backfired on account of the soldier's loyalty to David and the nation of Israel, David had him killed. So David was not only an adulterer, but a murderer, too. Yet David is remembered in the New Testament as "a man after [God's] heart." His obedience and heart for God, not the times in which he blew it, defined the whole of his life.

Centuries later, when Paul spoke to the men of Antioch, he didn't call David "a man who was *once* after God's heart." Nor did he refer to David as "the man God was fond of before he really messed up." No, God preserved David's legacy as one of obedience and commitment.

Wouldn't it be great if that were *our* legacy, too?

He Knows My Heart

I was thinking recently about the kind of legacy I will leave someday. That afternoon, I took a long walk near some homes by a lake because I was discouraged that after so many years as a follower of Christ, I still mess up in some of the stupidest ways. *Aren't I beyond this?* I scolded myself. *Wretched woman that I am!* I felt complacent and compromised. I was looking back at times in my life when my passion for God burned brighter and my service for Him seemed much more fruitful.

God, I want the last part of my life to be stronger than the first, I prayed. *I want You to define my life by the years I obeyed You, served You with passion, desired You more than anything.* I felt saddened, as if I'd lost something through the years or perhaps I wasn't who I used to be when it came to my heart for God.

Suddenly a child's voice interrupted my thoughts. I looked up the hill toward the sound and saw a little blond girl, about five years old, in a red ruffled dress. She was holding onto a wrought iron fence, swaying back and forth, and singing a song to Jesus that I used to sing when I was her age.

Tears came to my eyes as I watched her sway back and forth and listened to her sweet song. "That was me, God," I whispered. (She *did* look just like I had, some 40 years ago, with her white-blond hair and red ruffled dress!) "You saw me back then when I played in my backyard, Lord. You heard *me* sing that song to You. You have seen my life—from beginning to end—and You are more familiar with my heart than anyone."

It comforted me to know that, in that moment when I was wondering if God saw who I really was, He let me observe a little girl, and hear her heart for Jesus, and know that as clearly as I saw and heard her, my heavenly Father has seen and heard my heart—and songs—all these years. I couldn't help but feel, in that moment, as if God was whispering to me, "I remember…"

Do you have a precious childhood memory of talking to Jesus or singing to Him? Did you, as a child, trust Jesus, but feel that it wasn't until years later that you really understand what it means to have a relationship with Him? Or maybe you only recently have learned what it means to trust in the Lord. No matter when it started, the sound of your cries to Him are as precious to Him today as they were when you first uttered them.

God told His people, through the prophet Isaiah, how He would never forget them:

> Can a mother forget the baby at her breast
>   and have no compassion on the child she has borne?
> Though she may forget,
>   I will not forget you!
> See, I have engraved you on the palms of my hands;
>   Your walls are ever before me (Isaiah 49:15-16).

Five years after this book becomes available, I'll be half a century old! That makes me realize there are probably fewer days ahead of me than behind me, and I want to live them in a way that truly matters. My obedience to God is more important now than ever. That struggle with self must be mastered. So I don't want to be a woman who merely obeys God. I want to be a woman on the edge for Him…so desperate to obey Him and please Him and do *all* His will that it becomes my consuming passion. That is my desire.

Would you make it *yours*, too?

Finding Your Spacious Place

I run in the path of your commands, for
you have set my heart free.

PSALM 119:32

If you are desperate to obey God in a certain area, He knows. And He's the only One who can get you across that abyss from where you are to where you want to be in Him. Complete these exercises so you can—with a heart that is free—run in the path of His commands.

1. Which of the "Living in Obedience" principles on pages 146–47 is most challenging to you? (Circle one below.) Next to each principle, list at least one way you can live it out on a daily basis.

   a. Let Go of Self

   b. Live Under the Spirit's Control

   c. Love One Another

2. Personalize Psalm 15 by rewriting it in your own words in the space below. Then repeat it back to God as a prayer for your life:

3. One of the best ways to live by the Spirit, and not the flesh, is to be filled with the Word of God. Look up the following verses, write them out in the space below, and then choose at least one to memorize this week.

Psalm 119:32:

Psalm 119:36:

Psalm 119:105:

Psalm 119:133:

Galatians 5:16:

Philippians 1:27:

Colossians 2:6-7:

10

Desperate to Serve Him

DESIRING HIS PLEASURE

If God has been generous with you,
he will expect you to serve him well.
But if he has been more than generous,
he will expect you to serve him even better.

LUKE 12:48 CEV

Twenty-nine-year-old Jenn is a confident, capable, and compassionate woman. One would never guess that she grew up on the edge.

"Ever since I was a child, I've had the deepest desire for a real father," Jenn told me recently. "My father despised me from birth. My earliest memories are of his emotional abuse, which continued until my parents divorced when I was about thirteen. Not only did he abuse me emotionally, physically, and on one occasion sexually, but he did everything in his power to make my life as miserable and devoid of hope as possible. Thus I greatly yearned for a father who would protect me instead of hurt me, love me instead of hate me, and encourage me instead of abuse me."

Jenn's dad was young and immature at the time he became a father. She happened to be the oldest child, and her father began to blame her for the sacrifices he had to make for his family. He taught Jenn's younger sisters to despise her as well.

"Any time there was any sort of light as I was growing up, the door got slammed shut. It was like living in a prison of hell for a long time. I never imagined I could have been happy and healthy and have a sense of myself."

But today, through the grace of God—who became Jenn's "Daddy" when she met Him through a personal relationship with Christ about four years ago—Jenn knows who she is. She is a child of *God's,* she will tell you—and she is loved.

"The most important role I possess," she said, "is that of God's child—His daughter. Through Jesus' sacrifice, God has cleansed me and brought me into His kingdom to receive His inheritance. Therefore, I am more than just His child: I am His *princess.*"

And what does this princess want to do with the rest of her life? She wants to *serve* her king—to not only accept all that the Lord offers her, but to take what He gives her and pour it back into His kingdom.

"God has spent the last four years repairing the damage done in my past. Now I am at the point in my spiritual growth where I am able—and ready—to consider the future. I must ask myself, 'How will I serve my Father? How will I serve His kingdom?'"

One of the ways she uses her gifts and abilities to serve God and invest in His kingdom is through Web site design, particularly for ministries, nonprofit organizations, and businesses that seek to glorify God through their work.[37] As a college student majoring in Web design, Jenn contacted me several years ago—after hearing me speak at her church—and offered to redesign and maintain my Web site. I have since hired her for numerous projects and am amazed at her ability, creativity, and joyful spirit.

Today Jenn is passionate about writing, Web design, and "doing whatever God wants me to do, especially if it falls within my dream statement. My God-given dream is to create, inspire, and motivate hope and happiness for those in need via the creative arts, particularly writing and graphic design."[38]

Jenn is an example of a woman who has recognized God's lavishing love on her life and has responded by being on the edge to serve Him.

Having been desperate all her life for a father's love, Jenn learned slowly but surely to trust God in the ways she always wanted to trust a father. "It has taken nearly all four years since I was saved for God to get me to a place where I can call Him 'Daddy' and consider Him my Father." But now that she can, she is consumed with a desire to love Him in return and serve Him for all He's done for her.

"I don't want to be just *a* Christian. I want to be God's *daughter*—His princess. And being a princess isn't just about accepting your rich inheritance and cruising through life. It's a position of responsibility to both your sovereign the King and to the kingdom. And I am determined to serve my Lord the best I can."

That's the kind of love that prompts a desperation to serve God. It's a feeling of indebtedness, a feeling of immense gratitude for the One who has given His all.

Lynda felt that kind of indebtedness to her Savior, too.

Serving Him Through Surrender

Lynda was at the place in life where most women begin to live for themselves. She became a single mom when her two children were approaching their teens, and she raised them through high school, into college, and finally, out of the house.

Suddenly faced with an empty nest, Lynda was at a crossroads: Would she finally get the chance to live for herself? Or would she seek God's will over her own and find the *real* path to life?

"As a single mom, it's never really your turn. It's never about you. All you have is time to cope, and nothing more," Lynda said, recalling what life had been like raising two children on her own for ten years.

"There was so much weighing me down, so much coming my direction every single day. All I could do was pray to God to give me the strength to get these kids to church and depend on God every day to get us through."

So when Lynda's last child entered college, she was faced with the question many women in midlife ask: What do I do now?

"Some women go nuts and have a midlife crisis, but I simply said it's my turn to not have to do anything. I don't have to chauffeur, to make it all happen. And in realizing that I finally had less to do, I sensed a restlessness. I knew it wasn't going to be clinched through a shopping trip, a new car, or something like that. It was like a thirst that couldn't be quenched." She was searching for what she would devote her life to.

"I've devoted my life to my two precious kids. What will I *now* devote my life to? I need to make sure that what I devote my life to really counts."

And instead of doing what most women would do—looking at what *she* wanted in life—Lynda directed her "What's next?" to God.

"As a single mom, there's so many decisions to be made and no one to ask. I always went to the Lord first because I had no one else. So by the time I was wondering what I'd do with my life, it was natural to just go to God again and say, 'What do I do now?'"

Lynda took three days off from work to sit on her front porch, read her Bible, and open up her life to God. She told Him the desire of her heart was to serve Him for all He had done for her. And in that prayer of surrender and commitment, it was as if God looked over the desires of *her* heart.

Lynda had always wanted to own a home in the country. And she longed to minister to women in some way. God put the pieces together between Lynda's desire to serve Him and His desire to honor her for what she desired. She put her house up for sale, watched it sell in six weeks, used some of the money to pay off her debts, then bought a custom-built country cottage just outside of Kaufman, Texas, where she now opens her home on weekends for women's prayer and reflection retreats. Kindle Afresh Ministries was born out of Lynda's desperation to serve her Lord.

"I think it was my own twist on a midlife crisis," she says.

Only it wasn't a crisis; it was her deliverance. Lynda took her restless season of life to God and expressed a desire to serve Him, and He honored her by making possible the sale of her home in Mesquite, which allowed her to pay off some heavy debts—credit card balances, her car, and two home improvement loans. The move also allowed her to drive to work, park downtown, pay for gas, and be able to begin helping pay for her children's college loans while living on a reasonable budget.

When Lynda contemplated the move with the idea of offering her new home as a weekend retreat center, people tried to tell her she was crazy.

"People told me to stay put, not rock the boat. My house was nearly paid for, so people said, 'You're good to go for retirement; why would you rock the boat now?'"

Lynda says, "I wrote a list of thirteen reasons this wouldn't work. But I was still convinced God was going to help me."

Like God's servant Abraham, who was told to go out to a place not knowing where he was going,[39] Lynda felt she, too, was trusting God with the unseen when it came to serving Him.

"There were times I resigned myself to saying, 'I don't know the details, but I trust that You're in control. And You are the One who is going to make this happen.'"

And God made it happen. He worked out every detail for Kindle

Afresh Ministries to be born. Two months after moving into her country cottage, Lynda held her first women's prayer and reflection retreat with a dozen women in attendance…from pregnant moms to grandmothers.

Lynda says she is living proof that God honors those who honor Him. "On the surface, a single mom with two kids in college cannot afford to be living out of debt and in a wonderful home in the country, let alone offering her home for ministry."

Yet Lynda believes she can't afford to *not* live for God and trust Him with everything. "He's the same yesterday, today, and tomorrow. If He owns all those cattle on the hills, He can surely come up with lunch for Saturday."

Trusting God to work out her future and put her in a place of ministry for Him has made Lynda live even more on the edge for God.

"I'm a much bolder witness for God than I used to be," she says. "When I go out to eat, when the waiter comes up and takes the order, I always say, 'We're going to bless our meal; is there some way we can also pray for you?'" When Lynda said that at a restaurant recently, the waitress fell to her knees, clasped the hands of the women with Lynda, and prayed with them. She had just discovered she was pregnant, and she was fearful for her future. Had Lynda not boldly lived on the edge and asked how she could pray for her waitress, she would have missed an opportunity to minister to a woman who was feeling desperate.

Lynda continues to be grateful for everything God has done in her life—from His provision for her family during the rough years of raising her children alone, to what she enjoys today. Recently she was reading a chapter in my book *When Women Long for Rest*—a chapter titled "Returning to the Joy of Simple Pleasures."[40] She says, "I had to put the book down and cry my eyes out for a few minutes. I have truly been allowed to taste and see that the Lord is good and sometimes the love and joy and abundance that comes pouring into my spirit is overwhelming. I cannot take it all in—it's just too much!"

The Bible tells us of another woman who was so overwhelmed with love for Christ that she couldn't help but serve Him.

Serving Him Through Worship

Mary of Bethany was a woman whom Jesus befriended. One day He came to her home and taught a crowd, and Mary sat as His feet, mesmerized by His words. Her sister, Martha, was scampering about in the kitchen preparing a meal, yet Mary realized the Bread of Life was in her living room, imparting words of wisdom that she didn't want to miss. Martha was upset that Mary wasn't helping, so she complained to Jesus, in front of everyone, and asked Him to reprimand Mary so she would get back in the kitchen and help Martha with the preparations. Instead, Jesus defended and commended Mary for her quiet heart and rebuked Martha.[41] What a loving manner He had toward Mary! How He understood her, unlike anyone else.

Then, when Mary's brother Lazarus was sick, she and Martha sent word to Jesus, who was a couple days' journey away, to come quickly so their brother could be healed. Jesus didn't come, however. He waited another two days helping and healing *others*, and Lazarus died during that time. When Jesus finally came to town, Martha ran to meet Him, but Mary stayed back at the house. *How could Jesus not have come?* she may have wondered. *How could He just let my brother die?* When Martha returned from seeing Jesus and told Mary, "The Teacher is here and is asking for you," Mary ran to meet Him, fell at his feet, and began sobbing. "Lord, if You had been here, my brother would not have died," she said, repeating the same words Martha told Him earlier. Jesus cried with her, and then walked her to the tomb, where He did something she and the rest of the world would never forget. He called forth her brother from the grave![42]

After raising Lazarus from the dead, Jesus incurred the wrath of the Jewish leaders, who wanted to kill Him. So Jesus left the area to stay in a place near the desert. Then, six days before the Passover, many people began heading toward Jerusalem for the feast. Mary must have sensed the time was drawing near that she would no longer see her Lord. She and her sister hosted a dinner in their home in Jesus' honor. She must have wanted to relish every moment she had left with Him. She apparently wanted to express her gratitude and love to Him, for she took an alabaster jar of very expensive perfume, worth about a year's wages—perhaps the dowry to be given one day to a man who would marry her—and poured it on Jesus' feet, filling the entire house with the perfume's fragrance. She then wiped His perfume-anointed feet with her long, flowing hair.

Mary's extravagant show of affection for her Lord stirred criticism among Jesus' disciples, who were "indignant when they saw this, and said,

'Why this waste? For this perfume might have been sold for a high price and the money given to the poor.'"[43] But as the disciples ridiculed Mary for "wasting" her perfume on Jesus, her Lord again not only defended, but commended her. "Leave her alone," Jesus replied, recognizing that when she poured the perfume on Him she was preparing Him for His burial. Jesus saw that Mary, perhaps the only one in the room—or in all of Jesus' ministry—really understood that He would soon be dying to pay the penalty for the sins of all who would believe on Him for eternal life. Jesus also told the disciples that Mary, in her extravagant form of worship and service to Him, was leaving a legacy. "I tell you the truth, wherever this gospel is preached throughout the world, what she has done will also be told, in memory of her."[44] Mary was consumed with a desire to serve her Lord for all He had done for her, for all that He was, and for all that He was yet to do for her in securing her salvation.[45]

Serving Him with Passion

Mary had grown to love Jesus, from sitting at His feet while He taught and hearing Him defend her when the rest of the world didn't understand what she was doing, to seeing Him express His compassion and then raise her dead brother from the grave. She could've quietly pondered those things in her heart and never talked much about her faith, calling it something "personal" that she didn't feel she could share with anyone. After all, there was a warrant out for Jesus' arrest by the time He came to have dinner with Mary, Martha, and Lazarus in their home just prior to Passover. Merely being with Jesus could've been dangerous. But the depth of her gratitude toward Him, the intensity of her love for Him, and the urgency of her desire to do *something* for Him caused her to serve Him in an extravagant way.

Is your love for Christ extravagant as well? Do you splurge when it comes to worshipping Him? Would you spare no expense when it comes to revering Him? Because of how He's rescued you, delivered you, redeemed you, and transformed you, could you live on the edge by pulling out the stops when it comes to loving Him and serving Him with all your heart? Here are some ways to do that:

Be Extravagant

Mary spared no expense in giving her all to the King. Do you give

Him gifts that are fit for a king? David, while King of Israel, once said, "I will not take for the Lord what is yours, or sacrifice a burnt offering that costs me nothing."[46] Does God get your very best?

Be Focused

Mary wasn't bothered that others didn't approve of what she did. She realized she had an audience of One. She had only One to please, and His pleasure she received. What are you doing to please Him that others might not understand?

Be Emptied of Self

Perhaps the most difficult aspect of service is to rid ourselves of ourselves! When we do things for others we so often conjure up their appreciation and respect. Or sometimes we don't. That can make us feel unappreciated or taken advantage of. But is it about us or is it about the One whom we ultimately serve? The servant has no rights. She merely serves the One who is in authority over her. When we are truly servants—when we are truly serving—we are not mindful of ourselves, but of the Lord Jesus Christ, whom we are serving.

Choosing Whom You'll Serve

So how do we show that kind of love and devotion to the Lord today? We can't physically anoint Him because He is not physically in our presence, as was the case in Mary's house that evening. But we can follow His commands to love Him—by loving others. We can put Him first—by putting others first. We can serve Him—by serving others.

Jesus told His followers, "No one can serve two masters. Either he will hate the one and love the other, or he will be devoted to the one and despise the other."[47] Jesus was not only telling them they couldn't serve both God and money, but that they couldn't serve both their own interests and God's. So who will win when you get to that place in life where you must decide what you will do with the remainder of your days?

I really believe the central question in our lives, as women on the edge, comes down to this: Whom will you serve—God or yourself? It's the same question we considered at the beginning of this book. There are two paths in front of us: one path—of serving self—leads to destruction.

The other path—of serving the living God—leads to life. Which path will you take?

Joshua, who led the people of Israel into the Promised Land after Moses died, said these words to them as they were faced with a decision about what to do next:

> If serving the Lord seems undesirable to you, then choose for yourselves this day whom you will serve, whether the gods your forefathers served beyond the River, or the gods of the Amorites, in whose land you are living. But as for me and my household, we will serve the Lord (Joshua 24:15).

Who will *you* choose to serve? Yourself and your desires? Or your God?

Serving Him over Self

My friend, Louise, is very aware of the fact she has two paths in front of her. She realizes, every day, that she can choose to serve herself or to serve her God. Louise has discovered that by choosing to serve God and not herself, she is on the path of life—toward a larger life than she had before. Louise and I joked recently about how serving God keeps a woman sane. I can't say that Louise serves God *because* it keeps her sane. But she will tell you that is clearly one of the *benefits* of her service to God. Louise has always been a woman on the edge, a woman desirous of an existence that is larger than herself. And thus, she feels privileged to serve a big God whose plans and purposes are bigger than her.

At 43, Louise is a mother, grandmother, and businesswoman. She is also a volunteer leader with the youth ministry at my church, as she has been for the past 12 years.

"I'm passionate about helping young girls," Louise said. The mother of one child—a son—and grandmother of two grandsons, Louise has never been able to have her own daughter. But she has become "Aunt Lu Lu" to many teenage girls. Louise believes investing in the lives of these young women will perhaps prevent them from making some of the same mistakes she made as a young woman.

"I got pregnant at 19, before I was married," she says. "I want to see these girls make the right choices with their lives. I love being a part of these girls' lives and I'm hoping to have enough communication with them that they'll come forward with the issues that are on their hearts, and they are doing that."

Louise is also a volunteer, along with her husband, in the start-up of a Hispanic ministry at my church. Her life is full with her and her husband both in children's and youth ministry, their full-time jobs, and now helping out with the Spanish ministry as well. But rather than driving her over the edge, Louise says her service to the Lord keeps her focused on God, not herself, which keeps her in a spacious place.

"We have to get outside of ourselves and do things for the kingdom." Otherwise, she says, we will become self-absorbed.

Louise's mother's family suffers from clinical depression and anxiety disorders. "Their worlds have become very small and collapsed. It got a little too close to me. Keeping your eyes on God and working for the kingdom puts you in a place of abundance and fruitfulness, not dwelling on yourself. It gets your mind off of yourself."

Just like any of us, Louise has had circumstances in her life that could have sent her over the edge. Her only child eloped a couple years ago and didn't tell her about it until a few days afterward. On the heels of dealing with no wedding for her only son, no preparations for a bridal shower for her new daughter-in-law, and all the things that stress out— or at least disappoint—a mother, she learned that her son had joined the U.S. Navy and was planning to move his family across the United States, which meant Louise's two young grandsons would move as well. As a leader in ministry, as a woman who had influence over many, Louise didn't have the option of falling apart, bailing out of life, or absorbing herself in her own problems.

"I could've been paralyzed by all of that," she says. "I could've been completely thrown off. I had my initial moment of shock, but then I stepped back, accepted what had happened, and moved on. The Lord brought me through those things and gave me the strength to keep serving."

Louise's service to the Lord is not an escape because it's always been a part of her life. But it does give her life stability. "It keeps my world larger," she says.

"I've known women whose worlds are very small to the point where they're examining and criticizing others' lives at every moment." Louise recalls a time when she was very active and productive but was garnering the examination and criticism of a group of women who had nothing going on in their lives but the drama of critiquing her and others' actions. That's when she realized that God has spared her from much petty drama by calling her to something larger than herself.

When Louise first came to know the Lord several years ago, she sensed Him saying, "Get yourself connected." Because she was a young wife and mother of an only child she knew she needed accountability, support, encouragement, and a life larger than her set of circumstances. So she connected right away with a church and a small group of believers who could help her through life's issues.

Today Louise's life encompasses leading small groups, whether it be for teenage girls on Wednesday nights, the women in the Spanish ministry on Sunday mornings, or her own work-related groups. "If you don't have certain things in place, your world will become small and it will crumble on you very easily. The smallest crisis will make you fall apart because there's no support system, no study [of God's Word], no structure to your life. You'll get caught up in a victim mentality."

But when you are investing in the lives of others, serving God and working for His kingdom, then the world is not all about you, she says. "I've known the huge blessing of having God put certain people in my life at each of those moments when I could've gone over the edge…people to say the right thing, steer me in the right direction, or just help me keep my focus." That accountability, support, and encouragement from others is another blessing and benefit of serving God.

Louise is aware that the lure of the Enemy is to withdraw. The Enemy says, "Don't go," "Don't serve," "Don't get involved." And many women her age are dropping out of service rather than stepping into it.

But like Lynda, Louise realizes the older we get, the less time we have left to make an impact for the kingdom of God. So why delay any longer?

Improving Your Serve

If you are one who can't say that you are serving God anywhere, I encourage you to enlarge your world and start down the path of life by choosing to serve God in some capacity. Here's a way to get started. And to help you remember these steps, each one starts with a letter in the word *serve*:

S—Start with the Basics

When we are faithful with a little, God will give us more. Without even knowing that principle, Louise started her life of ministry with the most basic of service. "When I first started attending church I asked someone, 'How do I become a greeter?' I was told all I had to do was stand by the doors and say, 'Hello.' So I did that for awhile." As she was faithful in a little, God gave her more. "Start basic, and God will take it from there," she says.

E—Expand Your Interests

We often make the mistake of thinking the only places we can serve God are in our church or in a parachurch organization. But serving God and others often happens outside the church, primarily because that is where the hurting people are. I joined an exercise class in my community nine years ago, when I first moved to the city where I currently live, and I have had many opportunities to minister to other women there. Just by showing up, asking questions, and listening to women, I have often found myself sharing Christ with them while having coffee. Get involved at your children's or grandchildren's schools, volunteer at their extracurricular activities, join a painting or pottery class, or find another way to meet and minister to people outside your social circle.

R—Request from God the Opportunities

Isaiah 65:24 says, "Before they call I will answer; while they are still speaking I will hear." That verse was particularly encouraging to Lynda as she sought God's direction for her life. He already knows where He wants you serving, so even *before* You call on Him, He is answering. In my experience, whenever I've asked God to bring someone into my life whom I can minister to, He does. Scripture tells us,

> This is the confidence we have in approaching God: that if we ask anything according to his will, he hears us. And if we know that he hears us—whatever we ask—we know that we have what we asked of him (1 John 5:14-15).

V—Venture into the Unknown (if you sense God leading the way)

That's what Lynda did, and God had something great in store for her. Lynda told me recently, "I was just telling a friend yesterday that I felt a little restless, and I didn't know what to make of that because the last time I felt restless, I ended up packing up the whole family, selling our house, and moving to the country! That little country cottage has been a blessing beyond description—especially my early mornings on the patio listening to the countryside wake up! I cannot wait to see what God has in mind for the next adventure."

Your venture could be joining a small group at church for more accountability, support, teaching, and encouragement. Or it could be stepping into a ministry to which you strongly feel God is leading you. Any woman-on-the-edge for God will tell you, "Don't be afraid to go where God leads."

E—Encourage Others Everywhere You Go

There really is something to be said of the ministry of encouragement. There are people around you everywhere who are hurting, who have needs, who could use a little lift. Remember Lynda's ministry to the waitress at a restaurant? Lynda simply asked how she could pray for her. As you become an encourager, you will minister to others perhaps without even knowing it.

Finally, we must maintain a daily prayer time with God to ensure we are effective at any service we do...and to make sure we remember who it is we're serving. Early on in her walk with God, Louise was encouraged by an older woman to start her day with God in prayer. "Now at sunrise, I start with God in prayer each morning. I still encounter what we as women encounter every day, but with a different mind-set. And if for some reason life gets hectic and that prayer time gets overlooked, God brings it back to my heart as if He's saying, 'What about Me?'"

Finishing Strong

I mentioned earlier that I have now reached the age at which I believe I have fewer days in front of me than behind me. That gives me all the more reason to focus on how I will finish my life on this earth. And I not only want to finish strong, but stronger than I started. That means my life must become less about me and more about God.

It's easy to become women on the edge when our world is about ourselves. But when we expand our world beyond us to serve the King of kings, life then takes on true purpose.

Lynda, whose story proves that living for God is far better than living for ourselves, offers this advice to women as they reach midlife questions about what to do next: "You now are freed up to live for the kingdom of God, to build *His* kingdom. Yes, building into the lives of your children is important, but when they leave and make decisions on their own, you have more time to build up the kingdom of God!"

Do you see the rest of your life as an opportunity to finish strong? Can you be on the edge to serve Him as Jenn is because of the way God has been a "Daddy" to you? Will you, like Lynda, give all you have to Him in service when the rest of the world is telling you it's time to splurge on yourself? Will you let God enlarge your world, like Louise has, so this life doesn't just revolve around you and your circumstances? Will you give back to Him after all He's given you? Become that kind of woman on the edge—a woman who is *desperate* to serve Him—and see how God enlarges your world, your heart, and your life.

Finding Your Spacious Place

O LORD, you bless those who live right,
and you shield them with your kindness.

PSALM 5:12 CEV

The path of service to the Lord leads us away from the edge and toward that spacious place of His embrace because our focus is no longer on ourselves, but on Him. Work through the following questions so that you might serve Him rather than self.

1. Prayerfully fill in the rest of the sentences below, indicating how you can incorporate the principles from pages 161–62.

   I can be extravagant in my worship of God by _____

   _____

   _____.

   I can be more focused in serving Him by _____

   _____

   _____.

   I can be emptied of self when I serve Him by _____ .

   _____

   _____.

2. Using the steps listed below (from pages 166–67), how can you become a woman who serves God and not self?

   Start with the Basics:

   Expand Your Interests:

   Request from God the Opportunities:

Venture into the Unknown:

Encourage Others Everywhere You Go:

3. Read John 12:23-26. What do you think Jesus meant in verse 26 when He said "Whoever serves me must *follow* me"?

How can you live and serve according to that principle today?

4. Read Romans 12:9-13. How can you keep your "spiritual fervor" for God (see verse 11)?

11

Desperate for His Touch

DESIRING TO BE COMPLETE

You were in serious trouble, but you prayed to the
LORD, and he rescued you. He brought you out of
the deepest darkness and broke your chains.

PSALM 107:13-14 CEV

Deidra never really knew what it meant to be desperate for God
until her 12-year-old son, Joseph, was killed on Mother's Day
nearly 10 years ago.

She was with her two youngest boys, ages 5 and 2, at a birthday party
and her husband was on a fishing trip when she received the call. Joseph
was playing with a BB gun with a couple other kids when they pumped
the gun too many times. It discharged, and a BB went through Joseph's
face and into his brain. He died within a few hours.

"It seems like yesterday, and it seems like a million years ago," Deidra
says. "It was one of those unimaginable accidents. One brief moment,
and our son was gone.

"At first I was just numb. Then I was mad. I kept asking, 'Why me?' I
didn't understand. I was angry at God for taking my son. I kept thinking
that I was a good person. I have been a Christian most of my life. I had
never done terrible things to people. *Why* was this happening?"

Deidra and her husband divorced shortly afterward, leaving her to
raise her two younger sons on her own. She had to sell her home and
move because she could no longer afford to live in that home with only
one income.

"It was at this point that I was totally broken and ready to give up. I
finally stopped *blaming* God and started *begging* Him," Deidra says.

171

She spent the next couple years crying out to God...desperate for His touch. Desperate to be healed of her sorrow. Desperate to hope again.

"It has been ten years now," she says. "God carried me through those years. I never would have made it on my own."

Today, if you ask Deidra about her life, she won't tell you about the bitterness, but will instead talk of the blessings.

"I feel very blessed," she said, recounting that her younger sons are both teenagers now who are followers of Christ. And she now has a "wonderful, loving, Christian husband." She also says that "God has turned my tragedy into an opportunity to minister to others."

"Now I find that God places people in my life whom He wants me to minister to. He is always putting opportunities in my path. I just have to watch for them. *He* is the miracle in my life."

Deidra's life, by any other standard, could have been called a tragedy. But God's touch turned it into a triumph.

Desperate for the Light

Crystal is another woman who was desperate for God's touch.

Born into a pastor's home, but a very broken one, she received Christ in her heart as a four-year-old, but by the time she was eight, she was crying out to God.

"Things were not right in my home. Often I was left alone, confused, in the dark, in a box, hurt, torn, and crying. That was normal life throughout my childhood. I found myself often asking the age-old question, 'Why do bad things happen to good people?' Fortunately I also knew that God was never going to let go of me."

Through the help of counselors in her later high school years, Crystal's heart began to heal. However, upon entering college, she started to rebel. "While I was finding out who Christ was, I was also finding ways to rebel against my childhood pain. There was a true fight between the angels and demons in my life," she said.

After coming home from college, Crystal felt as if she were trapped in a box all over again and rebelled even more. "The worst part of it all was that I was a leader in my church for young teenage women—a mentor and teacher for them."

About four years ago, Crystal attended a young adult retreat, desperate for God's touch. "We had a night of prayer for as long as we needed, and as

I went to each prayer station, my eyes flooded with tears as God revealed my impurities. I began to realize I was being a hypocrite, just like what I saw in my own family as I was growing up." She describes that evening as her "face-to-face experience with God," because later that evening one of the women said to her, "Crystal, your face is glowing. I know you met with God." Another woman told her, "I saw you having a hard time at each station, but something told me *not* to touch you." Apparently God was the One who was allowing Crystal to be touched by *Him*.

Crystal's life turned 180 degrees since then, and she has only wanted God's touch—and direction—in her life ever since.

"My life has been full of rejections in every way, shape, and form, but God has *never* rejected me and continues to love me for who I am. He continues to give me a hope for the future. I owe my entire life to Him and am always desperate for Him, especially when I'm feeling alone in this world."

Listen to Crystal's heart for God in the song she wrote to Him one day while reflecting on who He is and all He has carried her through:

> Take all of me, Lord, and make me Your woman…
> A woman after Your own heart.
> Take my life and make it Yours
> That I may radiate Your life through mine.
> Continue to grasp Your child and hold her up
> To everything You have and will raise her up to be.
> Let your light shine through Your woman, Your child, Your servant.

Once desperate for God's touch, Crystal is now firmly in His grip.

Desperate for His Presence

In the Bible, we read of others who were desperate for God's touch and it showed in their songs as well:

- The sons of Korah sang, "As the deer pants for streams of water, so my soul pants for you, O God. My soul thirsts for God, for the living God. When can I go and meet with God?" (Psalm 42:1-2).

- David sang, "Answer me when I call to you, O my righteous God. Give me relief from my distress; be merciful to me and hear my prayer" (Psalm 4:1). And elsewhere, he wrote, "O God, you are my God, earnestly I seek you; my soul thirsts for you, my body longs for you, in a dry and weary land where there is no water" (Psalm 63:1).

- Asaph sang, "Save me, O God, for the waters have come up to my neck. I sink in the miry depths where there is no foot-hold...I am worn out calling for help; my throat is parched. My eyes fail, looking for my God" (Psalm 69:1-3). And later he sang to his Deliverer, "Whom have I in heaven but you? And earth has nothing I desire besides you. My flesh and my heart may fail, but God is the strength of my heart and my portion forever" (Psalm 73:25-26).

Desperate for Healing

There are many songs of desperation in the Bible, all written by men. But one of the people in Scripture whom I believe was most desperate for God was a woman—a woman whose desire to be healed became her driving obsession. She would stop at nothing to just *touch* Him.

We don't know her name or where she was from. We only know her condition, and it was a horrible one: she had been bleeding for *12 years*. She may have had a menstrual or uterine disorder, but whatever it was, her hemorrhaging made her ritually unclean under Jewish law and therefore, most likely a social outcast.[48] She couldn't touch—or be touched—by anyone or they would be considered unclean as well. What a lonely, isolated, affection-starved existence she must've lived! Broken as a person, emotionally and physically, she was also broken financially. Scripture tells us "she had suffered a great deal under the care of many doctors and had spent all she had, yet instead of getting better she grew worse."[49] At her wits' end—physically, emotionally, and financially—she was desperate to be healed and freed from this illness that held her in bondage.

This broken woman had no doubt heard of Jesus of Nazareth and how He healed the lame, blind, and paralyzed; cast out demons; and even raised people from the dead. And she believed if she just *touched* Jesus, she could be healed, too. She must have realized the scorn and perhaps punishment she would receive for touching Jesus and making Him unclean, per Jewish law. But in spite of her fear, she took the risk.

She had no other choice. With her eyes fixed on Jesus, she worked her way through the crowd, bumping and stumbling, and finally managed to reach out and touch the edge of His clothing. And just as she believed, that touch was enough to heal her. Immediately she felt the bleeding stop as Christ's power surged through her. And she, for the first time in years, felt the relief of knowing she had been released from her suffering.

When Jesus realized that power had gone out from Him, He turned around in the crowd and asked who touched Him. His disciples thought it a ridiculous question. Jesus was surrounded by a crowd, and everyone was bumping Him or inadvertently brushing up against Him. Some were probably even reaching out to touch this famous man who claimed to be the Messiah. But *her* touch was different. Jesus knew He had been touched intentionally by a woman who had faith that if she just touched Him, she would be healed. And His power met her need.

When Jesus looked around to see who would admit to touching Him, the woman fell at his feet and, trembling with fear, told Him everything—how long she had suffered, how no one else had been able to help her, how she hoped to just touch Him and be healed, and how the slightest touch of His garment actually had healed her. Jesus' compassionate response to her was, "Daughter, your faith has healed you. Go in peace and be freed from your suffering."[50] Her *faith* healed her—her faith, which resulted in her desperation to touch the only One who could make her whole.

It's interesting that both Deidra and Crystal initially blamed God for their wounds. Not until after they got over their bitterness and cried out to God were they truly healed. This woman, who was desperate to touch Jesus, didn't stay home and blame God for her bitter circumstances. She instead put her pride on the line and reached out to Him. She wanted nothing more than to be healed, and she wasn't going to let anyone or anything keep her from getting to Jesus.

The Power of His Touch

Can you relate to wanting Jesus' touch so badly that you're willing to do *anything* to get it? Perhaps not. If we are honest with ourselves, most of us will admit that we would long for His touch more if we really thought we needed it. We tend to think that we only need God's touch when we're physically ill. But, we can need His touch because of some emotional pain in our life that is eating away at us, or because of sin that has ravaged through us and made us spiritually unhealthy, or because of hurt or bitterness that has gone unchecked. What ongoing issues in *your* life cause you to need His touch? Or, what issues have you lived with for so long that you've resigned yourself to never being healed or completely freed?

As I was writing this chapter, I spent some time asking God to show me ways in which I need His touch...ways in which I am suffering from infirmities but may not even realize it. I have included here the inventory—or checkup—that I allowed God to do on my heart. Take some time to prayerfully read through this section so God can reveal to you any "infirmities" He's been wanting to heal *you* of:

- **Has my heart grown complacent toward my God?** Do I claim to love Him yet allow other desires to rule my heart? *If so, remove the idols from my heart, Lord Jesus, so that You alone reign on the throne of my heart and command my utmost affections.*

- **Do I possess a critical spirit**, ever aware of what others around me are *not* doing right, rather than seeking to encourage them, even in their mistakes? Do my words tear down or do they build up? *O Lord God, break me in such a way that I may no longer break down others, but only build them up. May your touch so rearrange my character that I am one who breathes life and courage into others.*

- **Am I displaying a love toward my husband** that "bears all things, believes all things, hopes all things, endures all things" (1 Corinthians 13:7 NASB)? Am I diseased with the sin of pride so that I always have to be the one who is right, always have to have the last say, always look to *my* needs and desires first? *Lord, touch me in such a way that I know what it truly means to die to self in my marriage and relationships.*

- **Am I harboring unforgiveness in my heart** toward any individual in my past? Am I accepting God's forgiveness of my sins but refusing to grant that same forgiveness toward another person who has offended me? *Oh God, purge me of a prideful heart that says my own sin is less offensive to You than someone else's toward me. Wound me with a reminder of how much I* *have disappointed You, and may that cause me to be overzealous in wanting to extend forgiveness and grace to others as You have extended it toward me.*

- **Am I holding onto pain from my past** in some corner of my heart so that I can pull it out at any time and grieve over it again, use it as an excuse for my sinful actions, or lash out at someone else in the same way that I've been hurt? *Redeemer of all things, touch my life and make me whole in You, so that nothing from my past dictates how I act in the present or future.*

- **Do I turn a blind eye to sin in my own life or in the lives of others?** Am I grieving over the sin in my life because of how it grieves the heart of God? Or am I allowing it, under the guise that "everyone makes mistakes"? Am I tolerating in others what truly offends my God? *Touch my life, Lord Jesus, and purify me so that I regain a sensitivity toward any type of sin, knowing how much it offends the purity and holiness of my God.*

You may want to take some time to journal your heart inventory and your prayerful response to God. Remember, if you could relate to any of the above questions and prayerful responses, Jesus is the One who can make you whole again.

As I was looking over the surveys of nearly 100 women whom I interviewed for this book, I found several common areas in which women, myself included, need the touch of God to be whole and complete. I also found that Scripture addresses these areas of a woman's life so that we can receive His healing touch. You can download this summary for free from my Web site at www.StrengthForTheSoul.com to use as a personal spiritual inventory, a reminder to tuck into your Bible, or a teaching tool with a small group of women. See if any of the following apply to you as well:

Five Areas of a Woman's Life That Need God's Touch

1. Our Hearts—So They Are Set on Things Above

Women often stress over the temporal—bills that must be paid, whether or not a man will come into our lives, if we'll be able to have a child, what someone is saying about us, how our body looks, and so on. At times we are more concerned about what the scales say than what God says. Our heart is more closely attuned to our bank balance rather than our life's balance. Yet God instructs us in Colossians 3:1, "Set your hearts on things above." If our priorities were in heaven and not on this earth, we would not only be happier and healthier, but less financially drained and emotionally spent. Matthew 6:19-21 tells us not to "store up for yourselves treasures here on earth, where moth and rust destroy and where thieves break in and steal. But store up for yourselves treasures in heaven…For where your treasure is, there your heart will be also." It takes God's touch to clear our heart of what this world says is important and focus it on the things above.

2. Our Minds—So They Are Transformed and Renewed

It's amazing how many women profess to know God and follow Him, yet their thinking patterns are just like those who are of the world. Scripture commands us, "Don't copy the behavior and customs of this world, but let God transform you into a new person by changing the way you think. Then you will learn to know God's will for you, which is good and pleasing and perfect" (Romans 12:2 NLT). Furthermore, God's Word instructs, "Fix your thoughts on what is true, and honorable, and right, and pure, and lovely, and admirable. Think about things that are excellent and worthy of praise…Then the God of peace will be with you" (Philippians 4:8-9 NLT). What mental anguish we would spare ourselves from if we would let God transform our mind and renew our thoughts to think as *He* would!

3. Our Mouths—So They Are Wholesome and Pleasing to God

Women tend to be communicators, and we can cause much damage with our mouths if we do not bring them under God's control. Whether through gossip, criticism, or unkind remarks, our mouths can serve as instruments of righteousness or unrighteousness. In Ephesians 4:29 we are told to "not let any unwholesome talk come out of your mouths, but only what is helpful for building others up, according to their needs, that it may benefit those who listen." God's touch on our lives can make us women whose words heal and encourage, rather than distract and destroy.

4. Our Bodies—So They Are Pure and Holy for Him

Are you one to worry and stress about what the scale says, how many calories you took in, and whether or not you can still fit into a certain size? God's command to us is "Give your bodies to God...Let them be a living and holy sacrifice—the kind he will find acceptable" (Romans 12:1 NLT). Yes, it is important that we keep our bodies healthy and in good shape (because we are His temple), but God says our greater concern should be to keep our bodies holy. In fact, God calls our bodily holiness our "spiritual act of worship" (Romans 12:1). One way we can keep our bodies holy is by dressing appropriately. People can tell much about us, and whom we love, by how we dress. Do we call attention to ourselves, or the God who made us? If the way we dress says, "Look at me!" we may want to rethink how we adorn ourselves so that others can see Christ through us. Can others see Christ in you, or are you getting in the way?

5. Our Emotions—So They Are Calmed with the Peace of God

There are days when, hormonally or just circumstantially, we need God's touch to calm our frazzled emotions and level out our lives. Philippians 4:6-7 says, "Don't worry about anything, but pray about everything. With thankful hearts offer up your prayers and request to God. Then, because you belong to Christ Jesus, God will bless you with peace that no one can completely understand. And this peace will control the way you think and feel" (CEV). A woman who is controlled by God's peace is not on the edge, but in the spacious place of His embrace.

I truly believe if we sought God's touch in those five areas of our lives, we would rarely have reason to feel we are going over the edge. For instance, when you get frustrated in a relationship, go back to the principle of letting God transform and renew your mind to think only on whatever is pure, right, lovely, good, and so on. And when you are about to lose it over finances or something that takes you by surprise, remember to not be anxious about anything, but to pray about everything... keeping a heart of thanksgiving for what you've been given. And when you find yourself desiring something you cannot attain, remember to set your heart on things above.

Desperate for His Ear

If you've found yourself in need of God's touch, here are some Scripture passages that will encourage you. Just as Jesus was compassionate to the woman who reached out and touched Him, He is attentive to *your* cries for help as well. Note the confidence we can have that—as we cry out to God for His healing touch—He will answer:

- "The righteous cry out, and the LORD hears them; he delivers them from all their troubles" (Psalm 34:17).

- "The LORD is close to the brokenhearted and saves those who are crushed in spirit" (Psalm 34:18).

- "I waited patiently for the LORD; he turned to me and heard my cry" (Psalm 40:1).

- "God is our refuge and strength, an ever-present help in trouble" (Psalm 46:1).

- "He will respond to the prayer of the destitute; he will not despise their plea" (Psalm 102:17).

- "All things you ask in prayer, believing, you will receive" (Matthew 21:22 NASB).

- "This is the confidence we have in approaching God: that if we ask anything according to his will, he hears us. And if we know that he hears us—whatever we ask—we know that we have what we asked of him" (1 John 5:14-15).

So how do we get His healing and completeness in our lives? We ask Him…we reach out to Him…we seek His touch, by faith. And Scripture says we will receive it.

Desperate for Deliverance

Psalm 107 is a song of thanksgiving to the Lord for the many ways He delivers His people. Listen to some of the lines of this song of praise, recounting *how* those who needed God's touch received His deliverance:

> Give thanks to the LORD, for he is good;
>> his love endures forever…
> Some wandered in desert wastelands,
>> finding no way to a city where they could settle…

Then they cried out to the LORD in their trouble,
    · and he *delivered* them from their distress...
Some sat in darkness and the deepest gloom,
    prisoners suffering in iron chains,
for they had rebelled against the words of God
    and despised the counsel of the Most High.
Then they cried to the LORD in their trouble,
    and he *saved* them from their distress.
He brought them out of darkness and the deepest gloom
    and broke away their chains.
Some became fools through their rebellious ways
    and suffered affliction because of their iniquities.
Then they cried out to the LORD in their trouble,
    and he *saved* them from their distress.
He sent forth his word and healed them;
    he rescued them from the grave
    (Psalm 107:1,4,6,10-11,13-14,17,19-20).

Four times in that psalm God's people "cried to the LORD," and each time they were "delivered" (verse 6), "saved" (verses 13 and 19) or "brought...out of their distress" (verse 28). In verse 20, we see *how* they were delivered, saved, or brought out of their distress. They were *healed* through the Word of God: "He sent His word and healed them, and *delivered* them from their destructions."[51]

In the Contemporary English Version (CEV), Psalm 107:6 reads, "You were in serious trouble, but you prayed to the LORD and he rescued you."

From this psalm, we understand that when we are in serious trouble—when we cry out to the Lord in our distress—He hears, He sends out His Word to us, and He delivers us.

The Power of His Word

So how does God heal us through His Word? A friend recently told me, "I'm going through something right now that you can't just put a spiritual Band-Aid on. The solution is not in a Bible verse." Of course it isn't. The solution is in the One who *spoke* those words in the Bible. The healing is in the *One* who heals.

As Psalm 107:20 says: *He* sent forth *His* Word and healed them, *He* rescued them from the grave. It wasn't Jesus' mere words that raised Lazarus from the dead.[52] It was Jesus Himself. "I am the resurrection and the life," He told Martha as she grieved over Lazarus' death (John 11:25). *He* is the resurrection...not just His words that called forth Lazarus from the tomb. *He* was the power behind His words. Because *He* said, "Lazarus, come forth," it happened.

The Word of God holds the same life-giving power for us today because of the One who spoke those words. We are told in Hebrews 4:12, "The word of God is living and active. Sharper than any double-edged sword, it penetrates even to dividing soul and spirit, joints and marrow; it judges the thoughts and attitudes of the heart."

And in 2 Timothy 3:16, we are told that all Scripture is "God-breathed" and "is useful to teach us what is true and to make us realize what is wrong in our lives. It *corrects* us when we are wrong and teaches us to do what is right. God uses it to prepare and equip his people to do every good work.[53]

Scripture is powerful because it contains the words of Christ, the One in whom the power lies. And it is able to straighten us out, and make us whole and complete because of the One who does the straightening, healing, and completing.

His Faithfulness Toward the Desperate

When Deidra quit blaming God for the death of her 12-year-old son and started crying out to God to be her shield, her refuge, her hope, and her healing, God was faithful and met her where she was. He patched up the painful parts of her heart and miraculously turned her pain into a sense of purpose and her bitterness into a blessing. And today she sings His praises.

When young Crystal realized she was being as hypocritical as she had accused her parents of being, it broke her heart and she realized she, too, needed to be healed of her hardness. That's when God touched her life and made her whole.

When my daughter, Dana, tore her ACL (anterior cruciate ligament) during cheerleading practice the summer prior to her junior year in high school, our first reaction was, "Why, Lord?" She had just received the Most Valuable Cheerleader award and had been promoted to the varsity team. She had worked hard to prepare for the competitions. Her coach had high expectations for her. Dana had given 100 percent. And she was badly hurt because of it. The ligament that held her right knee in place was completely severed, and surgery (and a minimum nine-month recovery period) was required before she could return to the team.

One surgery and seven months later—while I was speaking in Atlanta and my husband was on a missions trip in Colombia—Dana got on a trampoline at her friend's house. "It took only one bounce, Mom," she ended up telling me as she limped to the car when I picked her up after getting back into town. I found myself asking, "Are You kidding, Lord?" when we found out she had torn the same ligament *again*.

But what we called an accident (or rather, *two* of them!) God may have called sovereignty. During those seven months that Dana could no longer jump, perform back handsprings, or even dance at the level she wanted to, she ended up picking up a guitar. Long hours in her room, with nothing else to do, resulted in her learning to play and sing and worship the One who allowed her injury to happen. Today, when she would have been in the full swing of cheerleading practice her senior year of high school, she is now leading not the cheer squad, but her church youth group in worship on her guitar each week. And instead of the Most Valuable Cheerleader award at school this past spring, she received the Top Student Award in guitar and was elected chaplain to lead her entire school in worship during chapel services every Wednesday morning.

God didn't answer our "Why?" questions immediately. Instead, He let us watch a transformation of our daughter from cheerleader to worship leader. He let us witness a process in which a teenager developed a talent she can use to serve and magnify her Lord.

I remember Dana's words to me after her second injury. "It took only *one* bounce, Mom." But I can see now that it took only *one touch* from the Master to put her on a path that would glorify Him. Through Dana's affliction, God was able to touch her and make her whole and bring glory to Himself.

Sometimes God's touch completely rearranges our life, as it did with Deidra, when she lost her son, and Dana, when she lost her ability to compete in cheer. But God's touch *always* brings a restoration, a healing, a completeness we hadn't known before. And with His touch comes a story of His compassion, His power, and His ability to work "all things" for the good of those who love Him.[54]

Is there some pain in your past that has resulted in bitterness that still lurks in your heart? Are you enslaved to certain fears or a sinful habit you feel you cannot give up? Are you crushed by broken dreams, lost loves, or heartbreaking failures? If so, you don't have to stay that way. Go to the Lord and find the beauty in the brokenness, the blessing in the bitterness, and experience the incredible healing power of His touch.

Finding Your Spacious Place

Some of you were locked in a dark cell, cruelly confined
behind bars...then you called out to GOD in your desperate
condition; he got you out in the nick of time. He led you out
of your dark, dark cell, broke open the jail and led you out.

PSALM 107:10-14 MSG

1. Look at the "Five Areas of a Woman's Life That Need God's
   Touch" on pages 177–79. In which areas do *you* need God's
   touch as well?

   Pray right now to surrender those areas of your life to God so
   He can make you whole.

2. Read the following verses and indicate the benefits offered
   you from God's Word (also called statutes, law, commands,
   decrees, etc.) and how it heals, delivers, or straightens you out
   in your time of need:

   a. Psalm 119:24:

   b. Psalm 119:28:

   c. Psalm 119:32,35:

   d. Psalm 119:98-99:

e. Psalm 119:105:

f. Psalm 119:114:

g. Psalm 119:130:

h. Psalm 119:133:

i. Psalm 119:165:

3. Do you have a story of how God sent His Word (from Scripture) to heal you? As a personal reminder to you, write the verse here and explain how it brought healing to your life:

12

Desperate for His Glory

DESIRING NOTHING ELSE

You are the one we trust to bring about justice;
above all else we want your name to be honored.

ISAIAH 26:8 CEV

It used to be that nothing could get Jill's blood boiling more than when she was misrepresented. She would hear something said about her that treated her unfairly, and that would set her on edge. To hear her words misconstrued, or to find that she'd been misquoted, misunderstood, or even unappreciated was devastating to her.

"I was wrapped up in myself—concerned about my own glory—and didn't even realize it," she confessed to me one day at lunch. It wasn't until she came to understand how holy God is that she finally realized who she was in comparison.

"Now I don't care what is said about me," she said humbly. "As long as it doesn't reflect on my Lord."

You and I live in this arena far more than we'd like to think. It's natural for us to want to protect our reputation—to promote our best image—at the expense of hurting God's. A beautiful event is pulled off at church, and deep inside we want others to know we had a part in it. Our children are recognized for their talents and abilities, and something stirs in us to make others know we received similar recognition when we were their age. Someone gives a report about us that is less than flattering, and we lose sleep planning our response. Or, we are asked to publicly share something God did in our lives and we refuse, afraid that if we get up in front of others, we will look incapable, nervous, or foolish.

Can you and I take our desire to be noticed, admired, or at least well thought of and replace it with a desperate desire for *God* to be glorified instead?

I remember being jealous one particular afternoon for the glory God should have received in my life. I was one of many speakers at a women's conference and one speaker, in particular, took credit from the stage for all she had done to help each of the other speakers—myself included. She proudly recounted how she had encouraged each of us "unknown" speakers and elevated us to the place we were that day, on stage alongside her. There was an immediate burning inside of me and a strong voice inside my mind that said, "It was *God* who did that!" I burned with a jealousy for the glory that God should have received that day and drove home heartsick and determined to *never* let that happen again. To this day, I dare another person to try to take away His glory in my presence.

Jesus was defensive of His Father's glory. And if you and I are to live as He did, we, too, must be jealous for the glory of God—to the point that we are willing to give up the glory we would like to receive and freely offer it to Him.

The Root of It All

Our desperation to defend ourselves, to justify our actions, to protect our reputation comes from a preoccupation with and love of self. The older I get, the more I realize that if I want to be more like Christ, I have to squelch the urge to defend myself or make myself appear better than I am. I must be all about *His* glory, not my own. And sometimes His glory is best showcased when I am in the background, covered, content to let Him shine instead of me.

In his book *A Celebration of Discipline,* author Richard Foster says, "A frantic stream of words flows from us because we are in a constant process of adjusting our public image. We fear so deeply what we think other people see in us that we talk in order to straighten out their understanding." But, Foster says, when we choose to be silent—putting the stopper on all self-justification—we are showing God and others that we believe He can care for us—reputation and all.[55]

There are many ways we undermine God's glory, perhaps without even realizing it.

- We stress over the little things—and the big things—and therefore doubt His ability to take care of all that concerns us. This speaks volumes to others about how big or little we think God is.

- We perceive God as less than He really is. He is not just our "best bud"; He is the Creator and Sustainer of the Universe, the Most High, the Holy One. Yes, Jesus tells us we are His friends if we do what He commands us (John 15:14), but we should never have the audacity to believe that we are on the same level as He is.

- We fail to serve God because we fear criticism or the feeling of being inadequate or not good enough at a particular task. But that mind-set focuses on ourselves and how *we* will perform and what others may say about *us*. We hide behind false modesty, and our hiding is an affront to God who is able to do anything through us.

God's glory isn't about our performance. It isn't about how well we are able to do something and then our acknowledgement of Him (with a smile and a finger pointed toward heaven) as we receive the applause. God's glory is about who *He* is...and we are seldom in the picture.

Requesting God's Glory

When Moses pleaded with God on Mount Sinai to go with him as he led the people of Israel to the Promised Land, Moses made a point of saying that if God's presence wasn't apparent or known, he would have no credibility as a leader, no hope of success, and that they may as well not make the trip at all:

> Then Moses said to him, "If your Presence does not go with us, do not send us up from here. How will anyone know that you are pleased with me and with your people unless you go with us? What else will distinguish me and your people from all the other people on the face of the earth?" (Exodus 33:15-16).

When God agreed to go with Moses, Moses then made one more

request: "Now show me your glory" (verse 18). God's response to Moses is awe-inspiring:

> The LORD said, "I will cause all my goodness to pass in front of you, and I will proclaim my name, the LORD, in your presence. I will have mercy on whom I will have mercy, and I will have compassion on whom I will have compassion. But," he said, "you cannot see my face, for no one may see me and live."
>
> Then the LORD said, "There is a place near me where you may stand on a rock. When my glory passes by, I will put you in a cleft in the rock and cover you with my hand until I have passed by. Then I will remove my hand and you will see my back; but my face must not be seen" (Exodus 33:19-23).

God is so holy that no man on earth can see the brightness and purity of all His glory and still live! So God, in His grace, let Moses catch a glimpse of His backside. The part of this story that I love is that God placed Moses in a cleft in the rock and covered Him with His hand to shield him of His brightness so that He could pass by him. That's where *I* need to be so God can be glorified—in the distance, around the corner, in the backdrop, where I can look on and catch a glimpse of Him, content to be covered by His hand as He shines, rather than desiring to be out there on stage, at His side, sharing in *His* glory.

Moses didn't say, "Let me *share* some of Your glory." Nor did he say, "Show me how to *have* Your glory." His request was, "Show me *Your* glory."

I believe we would be much less on the edge if we were satisfied with watching God shine rather than trying to be the ones who shine. And when we truly learn what it means to let Him shine, He has a way of allowing us opportunities to let Him shine through us even more.

Responding to God's Glory

Here are some ways we can respond to God so He is glorified:

We Are to Respond to Him in Fear

In Scripture, we see several examples of the appropriate response to the holiness of God, and it is *fear*. Not just reverence. Not just respect.

But *fear*. In fact, in several places throughout Scripture, God *commands* His people to fear Him.

I've often heard women attempt to explain this away in their small group Bible studies. "We aren't supposed to *fear* God; we're supposed to respect Him," they reason. I dare to differ. A woman I was discipling once told me, "I don't *fear* God. I don't think He would want me to fear Him. I respect Him. But I don't fear Him." We spent the rest of our time together that day looking at examples in Scripture of those who *feared* God and pleased Him by it. I was able to convince her that respect for God is not enough. He wants a trembling in us when it comes to His glory and His power and His commands. It is a trembling that will make us respond to Him appropriately.

When I was in college, my friend Joani gave me the best definition I've heard for the fear of God: *The fear of God is a wholesome dread of ever displeasing the Lord.* That definition encompasses more than respect; it implies an absolute dread of disappointing Him. And to fear disappointing God speaks of love—loving Him so much I fear disappointing Him, just as I would fear disappointing my husband. In my marriage, the fear is not in the *punishment* from disappointing my husband, but in the consequences that disappointing my spouse might have on our relationship. The same applies to our relationship with God, but on an even greater scale. I fear disappointing God and grieving His heart because of how it would affect our relationship. I also fear disappointing a holy, righteous God just like I would fear disappointing someone who is in authority over me.

We Are to Respond to Him in Reverence

Israel's King David, who was known as a man after God's own heart, had a zeal for God's glory. On one occasion, when God told David to build an altar and make sacrifices to Him for a sin David had committed—a sin that resulted in a three-day plague upon the nation of Israel—David was offered an opportunity to take a shortcut in regard to the offering. A man who owned the property on which David wanted to build the altar offered to *give* David the site—as well as all of the materials needed to make the offerings to the Lord.[56] *What a blessing!* you and I might think. God's provision! But David looked at it differently. Here is his God-fearing, reverent response:

"No, I insist on paying the full price. I will not take for the LORD what is yours, or sacrifice a burnt offering that costs me nothing."

So David paid...six hundred shekels [about 15 pounds] of gold for the site. David built an altar to the LORD there and sacrificed burnt offerings and fellowship offerings. He called on the LORD, and the LORD answered him with fire from heaven on the altar of burnt offering (1 Chronicles 21:24-25).

Whoa! David was so determined to glorify God that he was convicted about offering anything to God that didn't cost him something. Oh, to be so wrapped up in God's glory that you and I don't feel an offering to Him is worth anything either unless it costs us dearly. How that would change our manner of giving! How that would change our manner of *living!* How that would make us women on the edge who are eager to see *Him* glorified.

We Are to Respond to Him Without Regard for Ourselves

In the Bible, we read of Saul of Tarsus, a Jewish leader in the first century who was passionate about persecuting Christians. He believed he was protecting the Jewish faith and pleasing God by exercising tremendous zeal to see that Christians were put to death for their faith. But the risen Christ intervened by showing Saul, literally, who He was and directing Saul to who he was destined to be—Paul, the apostle and bondservant of Jesus Christ, founder of many of the early Christian churches, and author of most of the New Testament. Once Paul's eyes were opened to see the truth of who God is, he became zealous for Christ's glory—to the point that he considered his elite Jewish upbringing, his education, his credentials, and his spiritual experiences *nothing* in comparison to knowing Christ Jesus. Paul wrote,

Others may brag about themselves, but I have more reason to brag than anyone else...But Christ has shown me that what I once thought was valuable is worthless. Nothing is as wonderful as knowing Christ Jesus my Lord. I have given up everything else and count it all as garbage...All I want is to know Christ and the power that raised him to life. I want to suffer and die as he did (Philippians 3:4,7-8,10 CEV).

And John the Baptist, whose sole mission in life was to prepare the way for the Messiah, said—at the time that he saw the potential of Jesus' ministry to eclipse his own—"He must become greater; I must become less" (John 3:30). John could've resented the Messiah, knowing that once Jesus came on the scene, he would be seen as second-rate. But he realized his whole life was about promoting God's glory, not his own. On the opposite end of the scale, the Jewish chief priests and leaders, upon seeing evidence that Jesus had raised Lazarus from the dead, feared a diminished stature and public image if people were to follow Jesus instead of them, so they began arranging for the arrest and murder of Jesus.[57] We can choose God's glory over our own and thereby choose life (as Paul and John the Baptist did), or we can choose our glory and honor and thereby choose destruction.

Mary's Sacrifice for God's Glory

Mary of Nazareth, the mother of Jesus, is one who chose God's glory—in spite of what it would mean for her life. And it cost her much. Mary was so completely absorbed in the glory of God and what was due Him that she endured a life of scorn because of it.

Mary was not the revered woman of *her* day as she is today among certain religions. Though she is exonerated for her position of bearing Christ, I imagine her life was quite rough. She was the mother of God's Son, whom the world rejected. Some scholars believe she was just a teenager—and a poor and humble one at that—when the angel Gabriel came to deliver the unexpected news that she would bear the long-awaited Messiah. Although Mary had a royal lineage (she was a descendant of King David through his son Nathan) and she was engaged to Joseph (who was a descendant of David through Solomon—and if there had been a king on Israel's throne in their day, it would have been him!), both of them were commoners, perhaps relatively unknown in Nazareth.

When the angel came and told Mary, "Greetings, you who are highly favored! The Lord is with you," Scripture says she was "greatly troubled" at the angel's words and wondered what he might be coming to say.

> But the angel said to her, "Do not be afraid, Mary, you have
> found favor with God. You will be with child and give birth
> to a son, and you are to give him the name Jesus. He will

be great and will be called the Son of the Most High. The
Lord God will give him the throne of his father David, and
he will reign over the house of Jacob forever; his kingdom
will never end" (Luke 1:30-33).

The angel told Mary the Holy Spirit would come upon her and the
power of the Most High would overshadow her, and the child would be
called the Son of God. At a time when her mind was probably swirling
with a million thoughts at this amazing news, her humble response was,
"I am the Lord's servant. May it be to me as you have said."[58]

Now I have to admit—if that had happened to me, I would've wanted
to think it all through. I would've wanted to first consider every possible
ramification, and then ask questions about every possible scenario I could
imagine as a result of a pregnancy by the Holy Spirit. *What if my fiancé
doesn't believe the pregnancy is from the Holy Spirit? What if I become an
outcast from the community? What if I'm called a nutcase all my life because
no one believes my story? Wait a minute!*

But Mary's response gives us no indication that she is thinking of herself. In fact, to the contrary, she proclaims that she belongs to the Lord.
"May it be to me as you have said."

Wow…no thought for herself. Complete submission to God. We
don't read in Scripture that she brooded over the effects of her pregnancy, nor that she was afraid when Joseph intended to divorce her quietly so she wouldn't be stoned for committing adultery. (She apparently
quietly trusted God while an angel appeared to Joseph in a dream and
cleared up the matter for him.)[59] We aren't specifically told whether
the community shunned Mary, but we do know that years later there
were occasions when Jesus was referred to as "the son of Mary," perhaps
implying that there still lingered a longtime question about the identity
of His *real* father.

Mary's humble response to the angel's announcement was marked
not only by submission, but also praise. When she traveled to stay with
her relative, Elizabeth, who was also expecting a miracle baby, Mary's
behavior was not one of brooding or analyzing her situation, but one
of exuberant praise for God. She ended up singing a song about God's
glory and majesty, while acknowledging her own lowliness.[60] As one
commentator states:

She took no credit for anything good in herself. But she praised the Lord for His attributes, naming some of the chief ones specifically, including His power, His mercy, and His holiness. She freely confessed God as the one who had done great things for her, and not vice versa. [Her] song is all about *God's* greatness, *His* glory, the strength of *His* arm, and *His* faithfulness across the generations."[61]

Perhaps the best indication we have that Mary's road was not an easy one to travel was the prophecy that she received from an old man named Simeon when she brought the infant Jesus to the temple for His dedication. After blessing Jesus, Simeon turned to Mary and said:

This child is destined to cause the falling and rising of many in Israel, and to be a sign that will be spoken against, so that the thoughts of many hearts will be revealed. *And a sword will pierce your own soul too* (Luke 2:34-35).

A sword did pierce Mary's heart as she knelt at the foot of a Roman cross upon which her firstborn son was being cruelly executed for crimes He never committed. Her son was hated by the Jewish religious leaders. And as He hung on the cross and neared death, there was no one there to support Him but His mother, her two friends, and Jesus' beloved disciple, John. It's safe to assume that Mary didn't receive much glory by being the mother of the Messiah. To the contrary, she was most likely misunderstood, possibly labeled, probably scandalized. Perhaps she became known as the "virgin mom who claimed to bear the Messiah." Yet we read nothing of bitterness nor regret on her part for being chosen to be the mother of the Son of God.

It takes a woman desperate for God's glory to have that kind of disregard for her own reputation, knowing that as long as God is glorified, all is well.

Are *you* misunderstood at times for the sake of Christ? Do *you* desperately want people to know the *real* story about you or your situation? Has God called you to something that few people understand? Ponder it in your heart until it becomes a burning fire within you...a determination to live for Him no matter what the cost and no matter what anyone else thinks. Be set apart. Be a woman with a mission. And, like

Mary, be willing to lose your reputation so that God might receive all the glory.

No Time to Waste

My friend Dawn Marie, whose stories are told in chapters 5 and 7, remembers the day she no longer wanted to live in complacency. She had already seen God's mercy and provision for her life when He withheld a man from her because He had someone better in store. But years later, Dawn reached a crisis point in her life and ended up in the hospital with an infection near her sternum. She was also experiencing an extreme amount of stress at the time. "I was trying to make my life work," she said. "One distinct day I put my hands out in front of me and said, 'Lord, my hands are open. You can take from me or give to me as You will.'"

Dawn Marie looks back at that pivotal time of surrender and sees it as the wisest choice she's ever made—to live for God, not herself...to take the path of life, not the path of destruction.

Today, Dawn Marie Wilson is the founder of Heart Choices Ministries,[62] which ministers to women on the importance of making the right choices in life. She encourages women to ask themselves, "Who do I want to be tomorrow? And how does that line up with God's heart?" Those are questions we must ask if we want to be desperate for *His* glory.

Today, at 58, Dawn Marie explains what fuels her continued edge for God: "I think the older you get the more you realize you don't have a day to waste. That thought can make you either stressful or really reliant on the Lord. To the contrary, most women wake up and realize they're a certain age and think, *I don't want to waste anymore time doing the things I don't want to do.*

Yet Dawn Marie constantly tells herself, "You don't have any time to waste, so don't mess around."

"I was playing it safe, and God was asking me to risk a lot more. I wasn't doing that at first. But since the day I sat there with my hands open, saying, 'What do You want, Lord?' It's been quite an adventure."

Showcasing His Glory

So how do we live that adventure of seeking God's glory and holding on for the ride? Here is a place to start.

Glorify God Through Your Conduct

In Philippians 1:27 we are told, "Whatever happens, conduct yourselves in a manner worthy of the gospel of Christ." Notice that word *whatever*:

> Whatever comes in the mail today...
>> Whatever is said to you at work,
>> whether you deserve it or not...
>>> Whatever grade (or disciplinary report)
>>> your child brings home...
>>>> Whatever your husband says—
>>>> or doesn't say—today...
>>>>> Whatever happens to you as you're
>>>>> standing in line somewhere...
>>>>>> Whatever comes your way in any given day...
> you are to live in a manner worthy of the gospel of Christ.

Furthermore, we are told in Colossians 3:12-14:

> As God's chosen people, holy and dearly loved, clothe yourselves with compassion, kindness, humility, gentleness and patience. Bear with each other and forgive whatever grievances you may have against one another. Forgive as the Lord forgave you. And over all these virtues put on love, which binds them all together in perfect unity.

If we apply that conduct—compassion, kindness, humility, gentleness, patience, forgiveness, and love—to all the whatevers that come our way, we will not find ourselves going over the edge. We will, instead, glorify God.

Glorify God Through Constant Praise

To constantly sing God's praises, recount His blessings, attribute your "coincidental" rescue to Him, and so on is to glorify God. First Thessalonians 5:18 says, "In everything give thanks; for this is God's will for you in Christ Jesus." Wow, that couldn't be said any clearer! The God who is worthy of all glory says His will for you is to express thanks in *all* things. That glorifies Him.

Think about it: What are the kinds of stories that truly impact those who don't know God? The story of the couple in the hospital waiting room who prayed and exhibited God's peace while their child was near death. The story of the mother who forgave the drunk driver for taking the life of her only child. The story of the people who lost all they had and praised God anyway. When we praise Him in *all* circumstances, we are saying to the world, "He is God, He is in control, and He is good, no matter what happens in life that I don't understand." God is glorified through constant praise.

Glorify God Through Courageous Living

My friend Rhonda (whose story I told in chapter 7) is a pastor's wife, speaker, and lover of God who helps women live deliberately. And one of her greatest joys is to take risks, live courageously, and speak boldly for her Lord.

In a coffee shop one morning, she felt a strong conviction to share the gospel with an elderly man and his frail-looking wife. Rhonda initiated a friendly discussion with Lowell and Eleanor, and learned that Eleanor had just been released from the hospital. Rhonda took Eleanor's hand and gently said, "Eleanor, I believe God wants me to tell you not to leave this life without knowing Jesus as your personal Savior." Rhonda explained to Eleanor that God loved her and provided a way for her to spend eternity with Him through the life, death, and resurrection of His Son Jesus, who paid the penalty for her sin and purchased a place for her in heaven provided that she confessed her sins and trusted Him for her salvation.

As Rhonda talked with Eleanor, her husband, Lowell, was very stoic and unresponsive. But Eleanor listened intently. Rhonda gave Eleanor a tract on how to receive Christ and told her new friend, "Eleanor, if you go home and confess your sins and receive Christ as your Savior, you will be forgiven. And when you leave this earth, you will go to heaven and be with Jesus." Eleanor smiled, through tears, and nodded.

Afterward, Rhonda continued to frequent the coffee shop, hoping to again see Lowell and Eleanor and inquire about how they were. But not until eight months later, when Rhonda got the overwhelming urge to stop at the coffee shop again, did she see Lowell again, who was with another man. Rhonda reintroduced herself to Lowell and asked about

Eleanor. Lowell, with tears in his eyes, told Rhonda that his wife had recently passed away. Rhonda then reached out for Lowell's hand and said, "Lowell, do you remember what I told Eleanor that day? That if she went home and prayed for the forgiveness of her sins and received Christ, she would go to heaven. And you can go to heaven too, someday, if you do the same and mean it with all your heart." Lowell smiled at her, and this time his friend was the one who remained stoic. As Rhonda left the coffee shop that morning, she couldn't help but look over at Lowell's stoic friend and wonder if *he* would be the one hearing—and receiving—the gospel next.

Rhonda lives in the liberty of knowing that she is not responsible for how another responds to the gospel (and no one has ever responded negatively to her, by the way). Yet she is faithful to her Lord's calling to share the truth about who He is and what He has done on the cross. She carries out this responsibility without fear of what people will think, knowing that it is God whom she seeks to please.

When we live courageously, speaking boldly for Christ, we glorify Him.

Living on the Edge—for His Glory

How do you and I become women like Rhonda, who courageously walk into divine appointments that "God prepared beforehand so that we would walk in them"?[63] Rhonda says that when she became desperate for God's Word, it was God who put that desperation in her to glorify Him. "Twenty-five years ago, God transformed me through His Word," she says.

Rhonda, who is now almost 50, says when she was a young mom, an older woman encouraged her to attend a Precept Ministries Bible study for women.[64] "I went mostly because there was free babysitting and I could be with grownups for several hours." During that study, Rhonda spent about five hours a week poring over the book of Philippians. "It transformed me," she says. "It made me aware of the Lover of my soul. It made me passionate for God when I had never been passionate for Him. He broke me. There was a brokenness over my arrogance and my satisfaction with being status quo in my faith, and I became broken over the condition of the lost [those who don't know Christ as their personal Savior]."

Rhonda says that when she went from just reading the Bible to poring over it and applying it to her life, it made a huge difference in her life. "It was like the first time you taste chocolate…you think 'Oh, I have to have more.' God's Word says, 'Taste and see that the LORD is good' [Psalm 34:8]. Once we have a little of Him, we must have more.

"Do I get lazy and out of the Word and complacent and have those days when I feel like I'm going to go over the edge? Yes," Rhonda says. "But God has always been faithful to place within my heart a burning desire to walk more intimately with Him. As I have pursued Him in truth, He has stirred within me even more of a desperation to walk intimately with Him. The more I sit and study His Word and spend time communing with Him, the more I desire it."

And the more Rhonda is with God, the more she wants to glorify Him. That makes her bold and on the edge for *Him*. Rhonda is not on the edge about her car breaking down, about not having enough money to buy a designer purse like the one her girlfriend just bought, about not being able to control her teenager, or about whether she'll have enough money at the end of the month to pay the mortgage. But she *is* on the edge for others to know Christ so that they too can live eternally and deliberately. "People want to know God," she says. "They want to know they are loved. How can I keep that from them?"

Time for the Plunge

Can you become so desperate for God that *your* life takes that sudden turn of seeking to glorify Him above anything else? Yes, I think so, too. So, let's learn to be bold, courageous, women-on-the-edge for God. Let's be women who are so passionate, so desperate for God, that His reputation and His image is what we hold dearest to our heart. Let's be women so wrapped up in His glory that we are singled out by Him as women after His heart, women who are highly favored among others, women who are pleased to do all His will.

It's time to take the plunge—to go out on the edge of what we didn't think was possible. It's time to live boldly so *He* will shine.

Finding Your Spacious Place

Because your love is better than life, my lips will glorify you.

PSALM 63:3

We become women on the edge in a negative sense when our main concern is to protect our own reputation. But when we become zealous for God's image—and seek His renown—we can live in a new kind of freedom that exalts Him without regard for ourselves. Work through these exercises to make sure Christ's image—and not yours—is most dear to your heart.

1. Which of the following responses to God is most challenging to you (see pages 190–93):

   a. Responding to Him in fear

   b. Responding to Him in reverence

   c. Responding to Him without regard for yourself

2. Prayerfully think about how you can glorify God through the following:

   a. Your conduct—what specific attitudes or actions do you need to eliminate from (or add to) your life so you can put God on His best display?

   b. Constant praise—what is one way you can remember to constantly praise God, rather than complain, about whatever is going on in your life?

   c. Courageous living—describe one way that you can take

a risk for God and live more boldly and courageously in your faith.

3. Read the following verses and record how you can apply each one to your life so God is glorified:

Isaiah 26:8:

Philippians 1:21:

Colossians 3:17:

2 Thessalonians 5:16-18:

Remaining on the Path Toward Life

Y ou've done it, my friend. You've made it this far. You've put behind you those desperations that can devastate and you've grabbed hold of the desperations that will liberate you…the ones that will keep you not *surviving* on the edge, but *thriving* in a spacious place.

As you continue to walk this path toward life, you will encounter circumstances that will attempt to lure you back to the path toward self. Keep your eyes on God and your edge for God by remembering that you were created to glorify Him and enjoy Him forever. Realize too that as you walk on this path, you will meet other women who are teetering on the edge, desperately looking for something to which they can cling. Walk them lovingly to that spacious place where they, too, can live for God, not themselves. Share the wisdom that you've found along this path, and help them continue to choose life!

You've been given the resources. You've been shown the road. Now go boldly into this adventure of living on the edge for God!

Notes

1. Genesis 3:6.
2. Kay Warren, *Dangerous Surrender* (Grand Rapids, MI: Zondervan, 2007), p. 22.
3. This story is found in Genesis 16:1-12; 21:1-13.
4. Genesis 1:26-28.
5. The Hebrew word for "desire" is the same Hebrew word used in Genesis 4:7 when God confronts Cain after the murder of his brother: "Sin is crouching at the door; and its *desire* is for you, but you must master it" (NASB).
6. There are several Scripture passages that instruct us to control our lifestyle, including Ephesians 5:18, which says, "Do not get drunk on wine, which leads to debauchery"; Romans 12:1, which instructs, "Offer your bodies as living sacrifices, holy and pleasing to God"; and 1 Corinthians 9:27, in which Paul said he beat his body to make it his slave (implying personal discipline) so he is not disqualified or discredited in his preaching and living for God's approval.
7. For more information on Overcomers Outreach, see their Web site at www.overcomersoutreach.org or call 1-800-310-3001.
8. John Piper, as cited by Carolyn Custis James, *When Life and Beliefs Collide* (Grand Rapids, MI: Zondervan, 2001), p. 109.
9. NASB.
10. Genesis 30:18.
11. 2 Corinthians 12:7.
12. 1 Corinthians 9:27 NASB.
13. John Piper, *Desiring God* (Colorado Springs, CO: Multnomah Books, 1986, 1996, 2003), p. 358.
14. In Matthew 26:31, Jesus told His disciples: "This very night you will all fall away on account of me."
15. From *Prayers for the Christian Year* by William Barclay, *A Guide to Prayer for Ministers and Other Servants* (Nashville, TN: The Upper Room, 1983), p. 268.
16. Sarah Young, *Jesus Calling* (Nashville, TN: Integrity Publishing, 2004), p. 207.
17. This story is found in John 4:1-42.
18. Elyse Fitzpatrick, *Idols of the Heart* (Phillipsburg, NJ: P&R Publishing, 2001), p. 23.
19. 2 Corinthians 5:17.
20. Lewis Sperry Chafer, *He That Is Spiritual* (Grand Rapids, MI: Zondervan, 1967), p. 32.
21. Psalm 23:6.
22. This prayer weaves together the following Scripture passage, in this order: 2 Corinthians 5:17; Galatians 2:20; Romans 8:1; Colossians 1:10-14.
23. *LOL with God: Text Messages from Heaven* by Pam Farrel and Dawn Wilson is scheduled for release in 2010 by Focus on the Family Publishers.
24. "Lead Me," © 2008 by Cynthia M. James, www.mcjmusic.com. Used by permission.
25. *When Women Walk Alone: Finding Strength and Hope Through the Seasons of Life* (Eugene,

OR: Harvest House, 2002), is available through Cindi's Web site at www.StrengthForThe Soul.com.

26. David's sin with Bathsheba is recorded in 2 Samuel 11; the prophet Nathan's rebuke of David occurs in 2 Samuel 12:1-10.

27. 1 Corinthians 6:20.

28. The Alliance for Eating Disorders Awareness, at www.eatingdisorderinfo.org.

29. This statistic comes from the South Carolina Department of Mental Health Web site at www .state.sc.us/dmh/anorexia/statistics.html.

30. From "A Cry for Mercy" by Henri J. M. Nouwen, *A Guide to Prayer for Ministers and Other Servants* (Nashville, TN: The Upper Room, 1983), p. 288.

31. The NIV uses the phrase "to strengthen those whose hearts are fully committed to him."

32. 2 Chronicles 16:9, in the New King James Version, says, "...to show Himself strong on behalf of those whose heart is loyal to Him."

33. Exodus 24:12-18.

34. Exodus 33:11.

35. Deuteronomy 34:5-7.

36. James 4:7-8 says, "Submit yourselves, then, to God. Resist the devil, and he will flee from you. Come near to God and he will come near to you."

37. For more information on Jenn's business, see her Web site at www.jennmurray.com, or contact her at jenn@jennmurray.com.

38. Jenn used my book *When a Woman Discovers Her Dream* to put together her personalized "dream statement" and discover God's dream and specific purpose for her life. For more information about the book, see my Web site at www.StrengthForTheSoul.com.

39. Hebrews 11:8.

40. This chapter is in my book *When Women Long for Rest* (Eugene, OR: Harvest House, 2004). To learn more about this book, see my Web site at www.StrengthForTheSoul.com/rest.html.

41. Luke 10:38-42.

42. This story is found in John 11:1-44.

43. Matthew 26:8-9 NASB.

44. Matthew 26:13.

45. This story is paraphrased, except in the case of direct quotes, from the accounts recorded in Matthew 26:6-13, Mark 14:1-11, and John 12:1-8.

46. 1 Chronicles 21:24.

47. Matthew 6:24.

48. *Life Application Study Bible* (Wheaton, IL: Tyndale House, 1991), p. 1740.

49. Mark 5:26.

50. This story is recorded in Mark 5:25-34.

51. NKJV.

52. John 11:43-44.

53. NLT.

54. Romans 8:28.

55. Richard J. Foster, *Celebration of Discipline* (New York: Harper San Francisco, 1998), p. 101.

56. This story is found in 1 Chronicles 21:1-28.

57. This account is found in John 11:45-53.

58. This story is found in Luke 1:26-38.

59. Joseph's point of view in this story is found in Matthew 1:18-25.

60. Mary's song is found in Luke 1:46-55.

61. John MacArthur, *Twelve Extraordinary Women* (Nashville, TN: Thomas Nelson, 2005), p. 119.

62. For more information on Heart Choices Ministries or to receive Dawn Marie's monthly e-newsletter, see her Web site at www.HeartChoicesMinistries.com.

63. Ephesians 2:10 NASB.

64. Precept Ministries International has a full line of Bible study resources that encourage in-depth study of God's Word. You can find out more about Precept Ministries at www.precept.org.

Other Books by
Cindi McMenamin

When Women Walk Alone
Whether you feel alone from being single, facing challenging life situations, or from being the spiritual head of your household, discover practical steps to finding support, transforming loneliness into spiritual growth, and turning your alone times into life-changing encounters with God.

When Women Walk Alone: A 31-Day Devotional Companion
Discover what it means to experience God's presence at all times with the help of this 31-day devotional companion. And face each day with a renewed sense of hope and fulfillment that comes from resting in God's love.

Letting God Meet Your Emotional Needs
Discover true intimacy with God in this book that shows how to draw closer to the Lover of Your Soul and find that He can, indeed, meet your deepest emotional needs.

When God Pursues a Woman's Heart
Recapture the romance of a relationship with God as you discover the many ways God loves you and pursues your heart as your hero, provider, comforter, friend, valiant knight, loving Daddy, perfect prince, and more.

When Women Long for Rest
WCindi invites you to find a quiet place at God's feet—a place where you can listen to Him, open you heart to Him, and experience true rest.

When a Woman Discovers Her Dream
It's never too late to discover and live out dreams in life. Explore God's purpose for you and make greater use of your uniqueness and special gifts.

When You're Running on Empty
Are you feeling run down and ready to give up? If so, then you're probably running on empty. There is a way out...with the help of simple steps you can take to restore yourself to wholeness and efficiency.

An Invitation to Write

Where has God met *you* on the journey through this book? Cindi would love to hear from you and know how you've been ministered to or encouraged through her writing. You can contact her online at Cindi@StrengthForTheSoul.com or write:

> Cindi McMenamin
> c/o Harvest House Publishers
> 990 Owen Loop North
> Eugene, OR 97402-9173

If you would like to have Cindi speak to your group, you can find more information about her speaking ministry at www.StrengthForTheSoul.com.